THE FIGHTER PLA

1. SILVER RAPTOR
2. SKY SHARK
3. BOOM BOOM BOMBER
4. DRAGON FIRE
5. FROSTBITE
6. DIABLO DEL CIELO
7. DRILL BIT
8. LOOPY LEOPARD
9. IRON NINJA
10. HASHTAG HURRICANE
11. KID SQUID
12. M.O.M.
(MONSTER OF MAYHEM)

Visit our PAPER PLANE PAGE

SQUARE ROOT OF SQUID PUBLISHING

BOOKS THAT MAKE YOU SMILE

SILVER RAPTOR

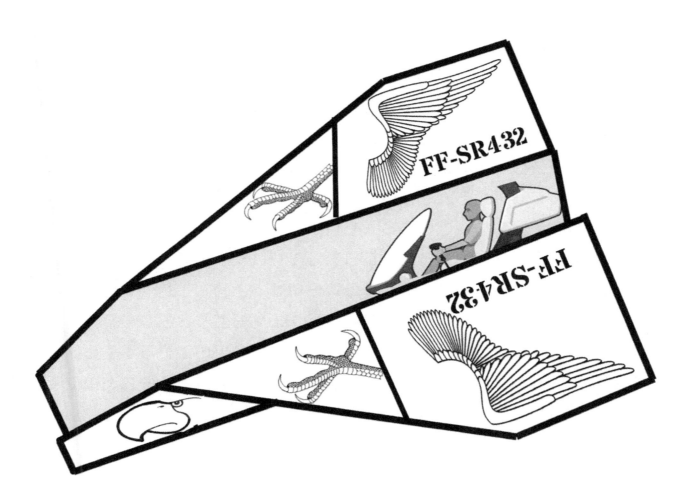

FF-SR432

TOP SECRET FILE

Name: Silver Raptor

The Silver Raptor is an extremely powerful aircraft designed with the concept of the raptor bird in mind. Just as these birds of prey hunt and swiftly snatch their food out of the sky or from the ground, so does the Silver Raptor jet plane when hunting for enemy planes. Once an enemy is in the crosshairs of the Silver Raptor it can shoot out its powerful steel talons, grabbing the enemy with such a powerful force the opponent is rendered helpless.

Superpower: The Silver Raptor's superpower is the ability to jam enemy radar and attack swiftly without being detected.

STATS

- Top speed: The Silver Raptor has a top speed of Mach 2.9, making it extremely fast. Its aerodynamic frame and small wingspan make it incredibly swift when in attack mode.
- Agility: The Silver Raptor can turn in any direction in milliseconds. With its multidirectional gyroscopic sensors, this aircraft can also fly upside down for extended periods of time.
- Stealth: The Silver Raptor has incredible stealth abilities, making it hard for adversary radar systems to identify it. Its cutting-edge technology enables it to snatch enemy targets out of the air without enemies even seeing it coming.
- Armament: The Silver Raptor has steel talons that shoot out and grab an enemy fighter in mid-air.

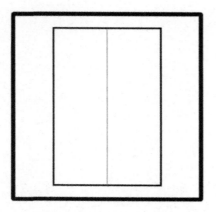

1. Fold paper in half then open again.

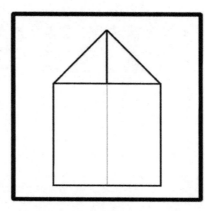

2. Fold corners to the center line.

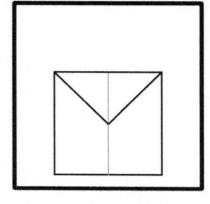

3. Fold the middle point down on center line.

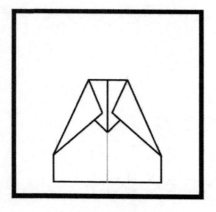

4. Fold corners again toward center.

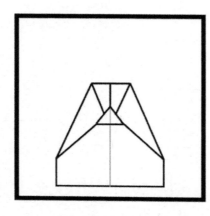

5. Fold the little center triangle upward.

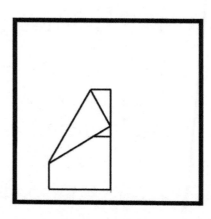

6. Fold in half and flatten.

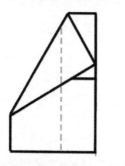

7. Fold a wide wing down where this dotted line is.

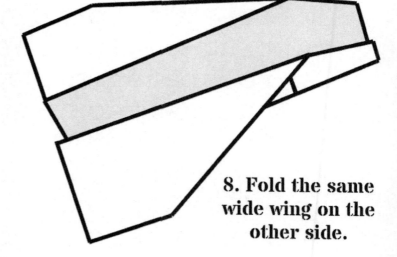

8. Fold the same wide wing on the other side.

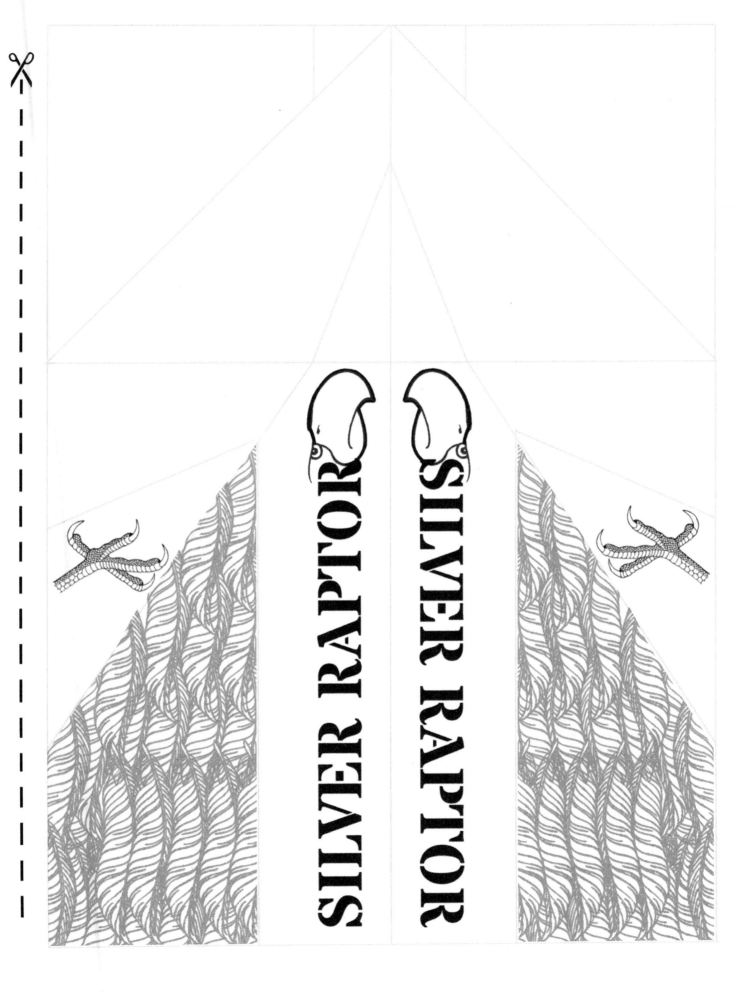

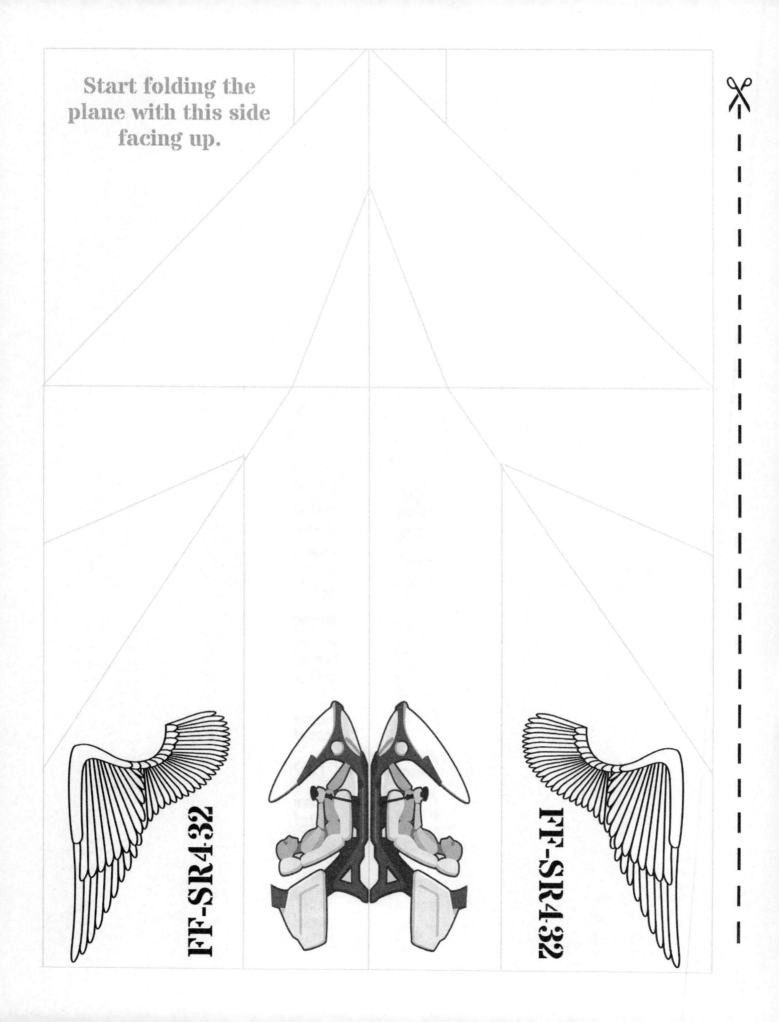

Start folding the
plane with this side
facing up.

FF-SR432

FF-SR432

SKY SHARK

FF-SS182

TOP SECRET FILE

Name: Sky Shark

The Sky Shark jet fighter is an extremely powerful aircraft and a menace to any enemy who crosses its path. Just like the aquatic animal its design was inspired by, Sky Shark has incredible maneuverability and can turn in all directions very swiftly. Equipped with advanced technology such as a high-tech computer system and an arsenal of extremely sharp metal teeth, the Sky Shark is an aircraft that will pulverize its prey in seconds.

Superpower: The Sky Shark's superpower is its capacity to detach its steel jaw to bite and snatch its enemy out of the sky in seconds.

STATS

- Top speed: The Sky Shark has a top speed of Mach 2.8, making it very fast. It can fly at great speeds because of its high-tech jet engines and aerodynamic design, making it difficult for enemy pilots to catch it.
- Agility: The Sky Shark's crazy agility and modern maneuvering abilities enable it to create challenging aerial maneuvers with ease. Often times completing full loops in milliseconds.
- Stealth: The Sky Shark has incredible stealth abilities, making it hard for adversary radar systems to identify it. Its cutting-edge technology enables it to snatch enemy targets out of the air with its steel teeth without enemies even seeing it coming.
- Armament: The Sky Shark has biting teeth that shoot out and grab an enemy fighter.

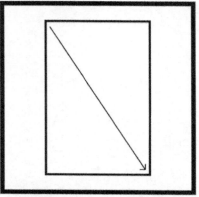

1. Fold top left corner to bottom right corner.

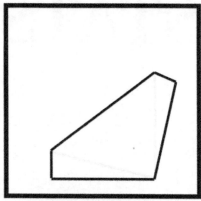

2. Fold flat to make this shape.

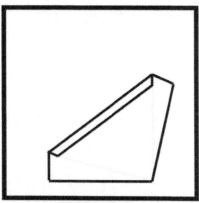

3. Fold over a small flap like this.

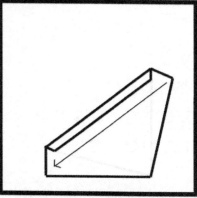

4. From the top right side, fold in half to the bottom left side.

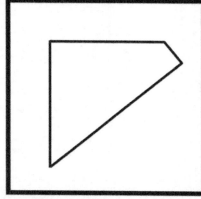

5. Flip over so the right angle is on the left.

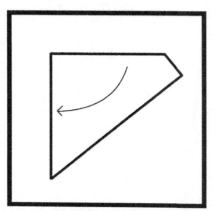

6. From the top right, fold one flap down.

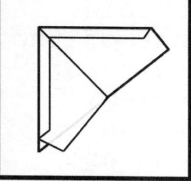

7. Fold flat to make this shape.

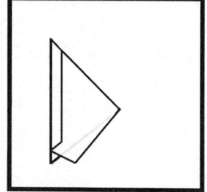

8. Fold the second flap down on the other side.

9. Fold wings on dotted line on both sides.

SKY SHARK

SKY SHARK

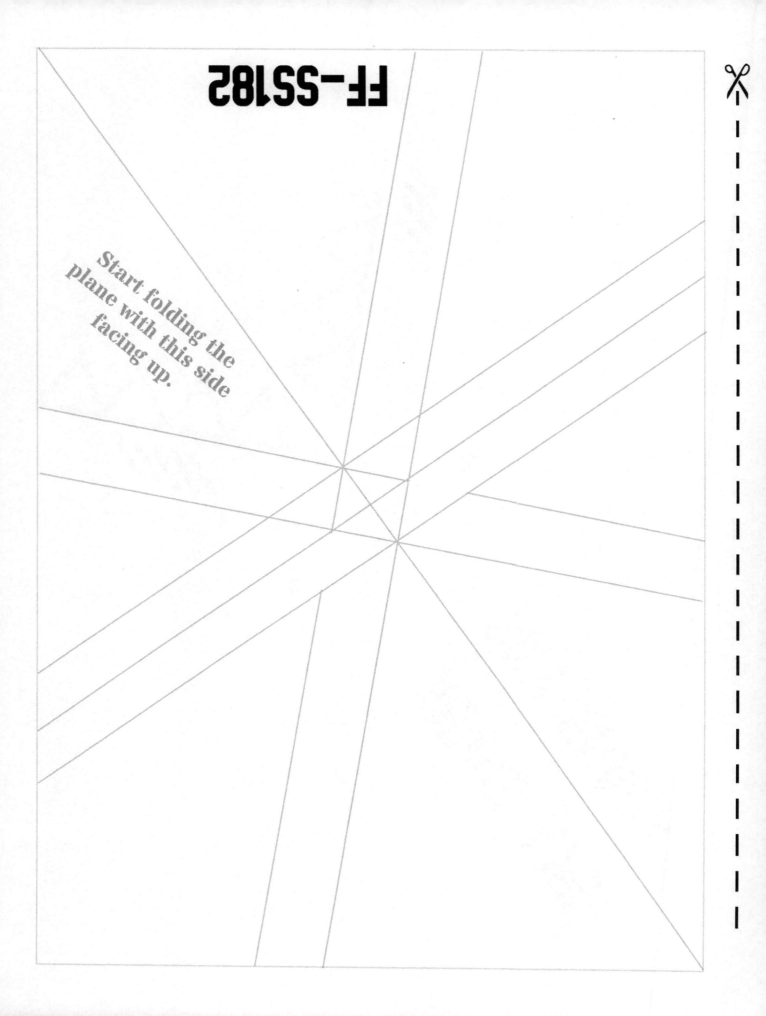

FF-SS182

Start folding the
plane with this side
facing up.

BOOM BOOM BOMBER

FF-BBB72

TOP SECRET FILE

Name: Boom Boom Bomber

Boom Boom Bomber was designed as, you guessed it, a plane to drop its payload on enemy ground targets. However, it is also equipped with turrets allowing it to knock planes out of mid-air. Also, with its rather large wing span and heavy nose, Boom Boom is able to fly at high altitudes for long distances without having to refuel.

Superpower: Boom Boom Bomber has the ability to turn itself invisible not only to the naked eye of enemy aircraft but also to enemy ground control radar, making it an indispensable plane in anyone's arsenal.

STATS

- Top speed: Boom Boom Bomber is not the fastest of planes with a maximum top speed of Mach 1, but what it lacks in speed it makes up for in endurance able to fly very far without the need to refuel.
- Agility: This aircraft was designed to basically fly straight although its two turrets have the ability to rotate 360 degrees.
- Stealth: With its superpower to turn itself invisible, enemy aircraft as well as enemy ground control radar will never even know it's there.
- Armament: Boom Boom Bomber comes complete with a bomb bay to hold a capacity of 50 units. It is also equipped with two turrets with the ability to rotate 360 degrees allowing it to stave off enemies.

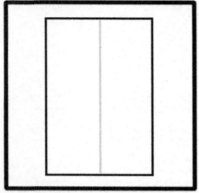

1. Fold paper in half and open again.

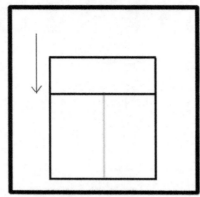

2. Fold top down.

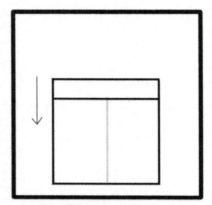

3. Fold top section in half.

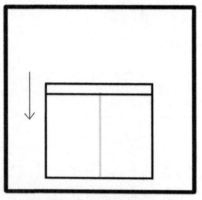

4. Fold in half again.

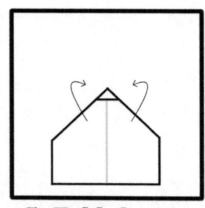

5. Fold the two corners back away from you.

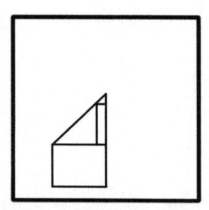

6. Fold in half.

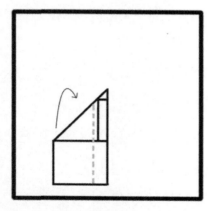

7. Fold wings down on dotted line.

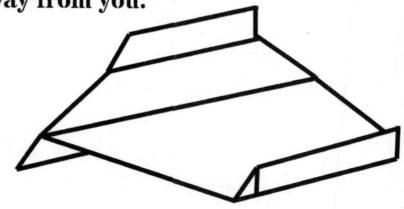

8. Fold wing tips up.

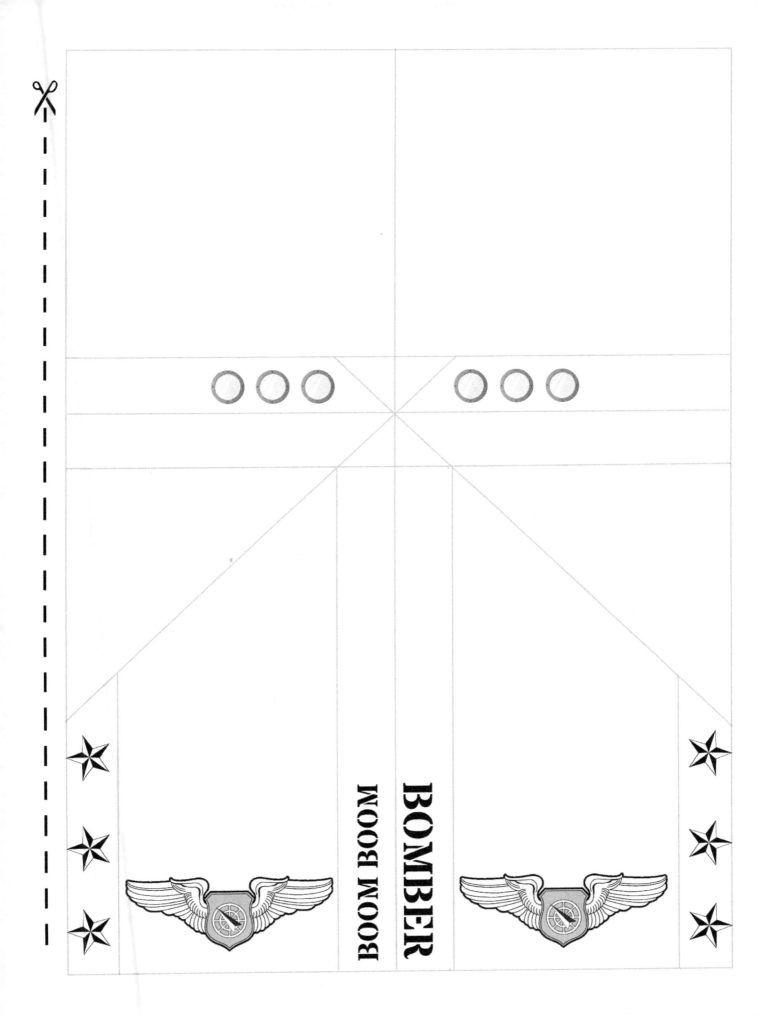

BOMBER

BOOM BOOM

Start folding the
plane with this side
facing up.

FF-BBB72

FF-BBB72

DRAGON FIRE

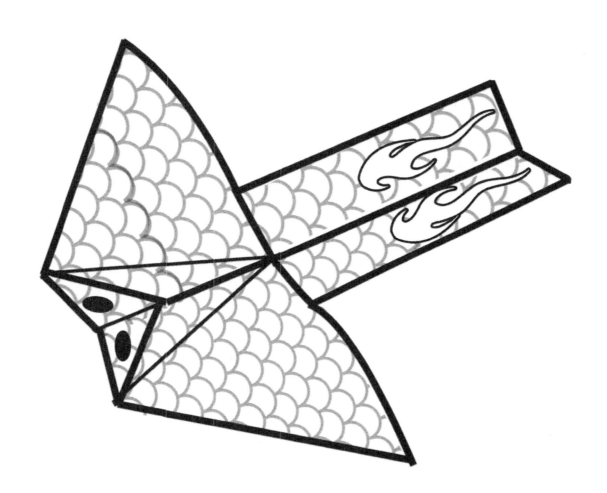

FF-DF002

TOP SECRET FILE

Name: Dragon Fire

Dragon Fire was designed under super secrecy to protect the technology from being leaked to the enemy. The overall design of this aircraft is bionic, meaning it is actually half real dragon and half computerized machine. This is a first in the industry and although it is a technological breakthrough, Dragon Fire is highly unstable due to the fact that it can think on its own.

Superpower: Dragon Fire has the ability to blow a fire tornado toward any enemy that crosses its path burning it to a crisp in seconds as well as metal scales protecting it from anything that tries to attack.

STATS

- Top speed: Dragon Fire is a very fast jet fighter that can fly at speeds upward of Mach 3.
- Agility: This aircraft was designed with a long tail allowing it to turn very quickly in all directions. Apart from this ability to move side to side swiftly, this aircraft can also take off vertically.
- Stealth: Although most of the time Dragon Fire can fly so fast as to not be detected by radar, because of its bionic nature the airplane makes grunting sounds often alerting its enemy to its location.
- Armament: Dragon Fire uses its fire breath to blow fire toward enemies. It is also equipped with strong talons and a whip-like tail allowing it to grab and/or knock an enemy plane out of the sky.

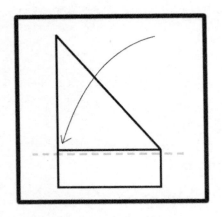

1. Fold top right corner down. Cut on dotted line and save the strip.

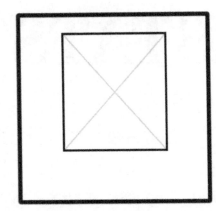

2. Fold top left corner down. Re-open to make an "x".

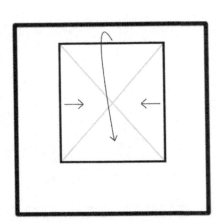

3. Push the two sides together and fold down top to make a triangle.

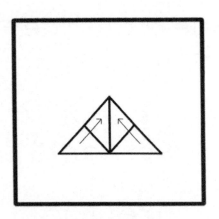

4. Fold up two small triangles to the center point.

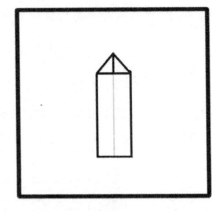

5. Fold the saved strip like this.

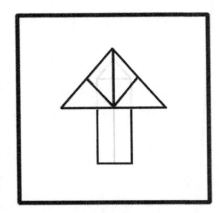

6. Insert the strip to meet the center point.

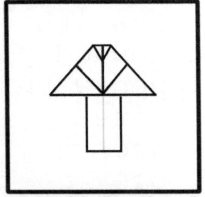

7. Fold the tip of plane toward you.

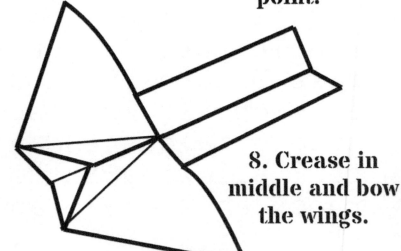

8. Crease in middle and bow the wings.

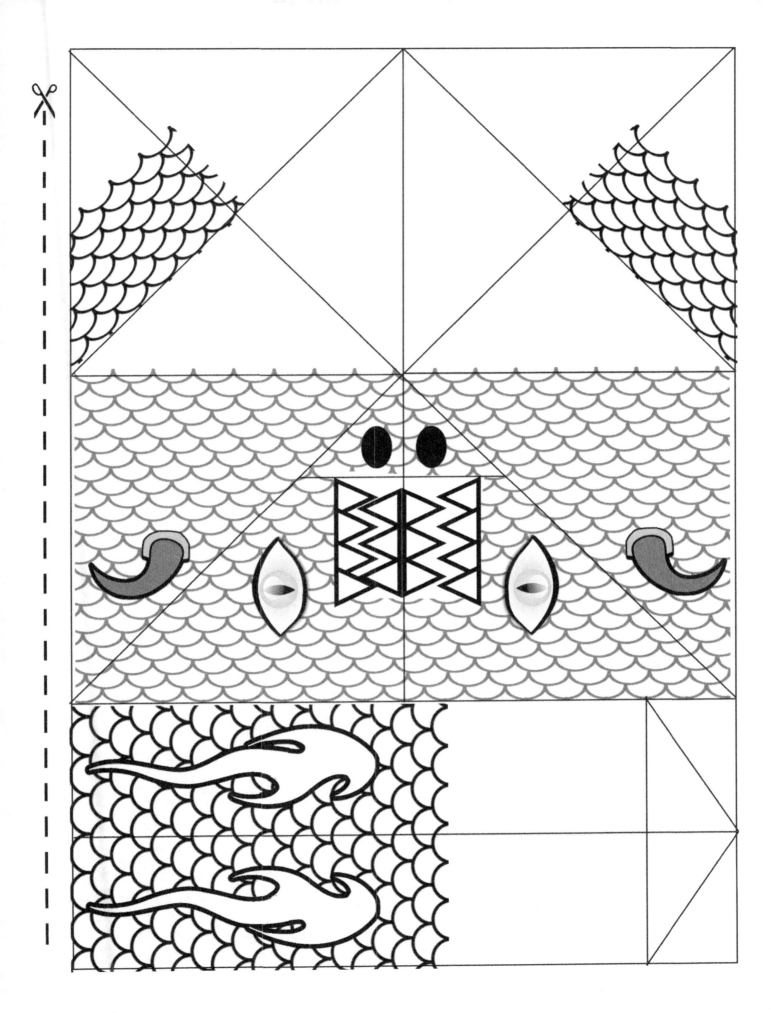

Start folding the plane with this side facing up.

DRAGON FIRE

FROSTBITE

FF-FB112

TOP SECRET FILE

Name: Frostbite

Frostbite in a jet fighter aircraft designed to withstand temperatures below -200 degrees centigrade. Its outer shell is made of super polymer titanium allowing it to fly out of earth's atmosphere where the plane is undetectable from enemy radar. It then swoops down on them from above at an incredible speed. Due to its ability to function in extremely cold climates, this jet is also planned for missions on Mars.

Superpower: Frostbite has the ability to quick-freeze any object instantaneously by taking moisture from the air and blowing it on said object, freezing it, rendering it helpless.

STATS

- Top speed: Frostbite has a top speed of Mach 4 while flying straight, however, can 2x that speed while diving from space to earth in a vertical descent.
- Agility: Because of Frostbite's slender body frame it becomes very agile in a dog fight able to pivot in any direction quickly.
- Stealth: With super speed comes super stealth. Also, because Frostbite can reach incredible altitudes as far as even space, enemy radar can't detect it until it's too late.
- Armament: Frostbite is equipped with a super coolant generating inverter which takes moisture from the air and freezes it around objects encasing them in an icy prison.

1. Fold paper in half and open again.

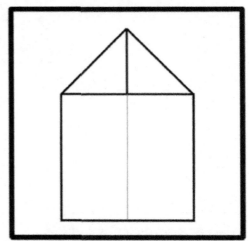

2. Fold top corners toward center line.

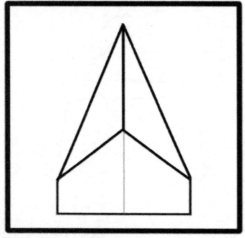

3. Fold side corners to the center line.

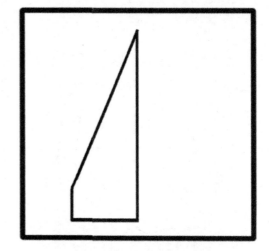

4. Fold in half.

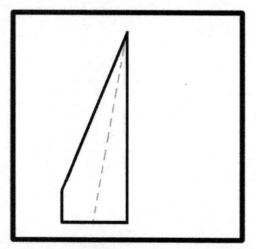

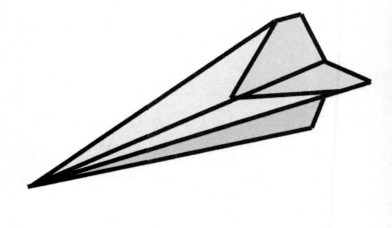

5. Fold the wings down the dotted line on both sides.

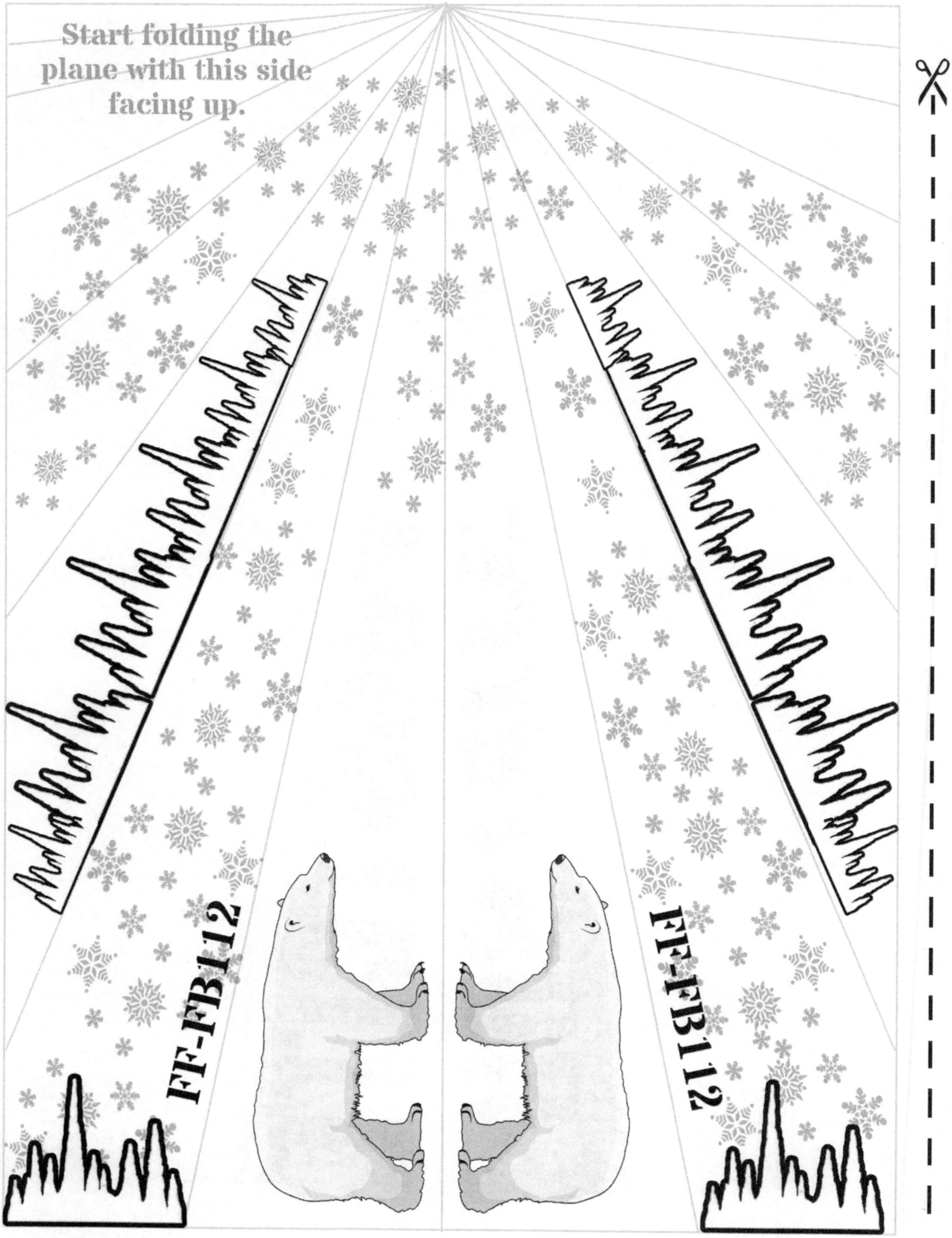

Start folding the plane with this side facing up.

FF-FB112

FF-FB112

DIABLO DEL CIELO

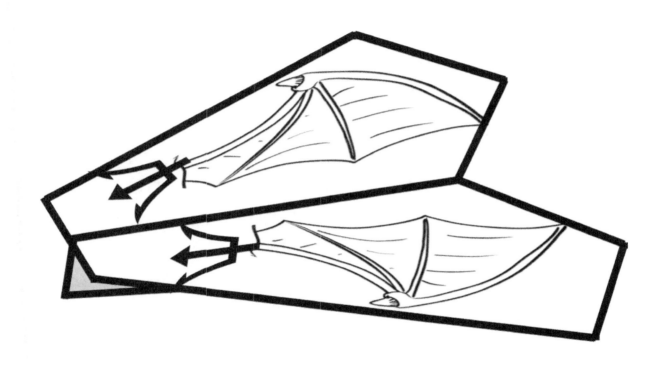

FF-DDC92

TOP SECRET FILE

Name: Diablo Del Cielo

Diablo Del Cielo translated to English means "Devil of the Sky". And this is what this aircraft is. Designed to smash enemy aircraft out of the sky with its high-tech gadgetry, aerodynamic fuselage, and heat-throwing ability, this "Sky Devil" is a force to be reckoned with. This airplane can reach temperatures so high it can easily melt metal.

Superpower: Diablo Del Cielo has the ability to not only throw heat waves at enemy aircraft but can also heat up its external body temperature so high that any aircraft that comes close to it will melt in seconds.

STATS

- Top speed: Diablo Del Cielo is not the fastest of planes but still pretty quick with top speeds hovering around Mach 2.
- Agility: The diamond-shaped back wings of this aircraft give it the ability to ascend and descend to various altitudes very quickly
- Stealth: Diablo Del Cielo is equipped with standard radar jamming devices, however when this plane heats up to full capacity it turns bright orange alerting the enemy of its location but by that time its too late and the enemy has already been incinerated.
- Armament: This aircraft is equipped with ultra-high rotational heat exchangers which take heat from the atmosphere to use offensively and defensively against enemy planes.

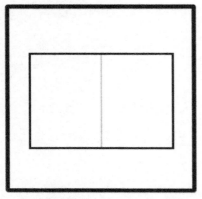

1. Fold paper in half the long way and open again.

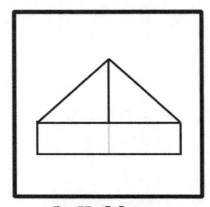

2. Fold top corners down to center.

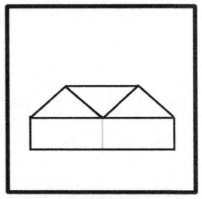

3. Fold the top middle point down.

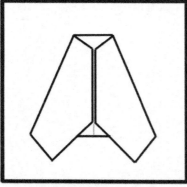

4. Fold top corners over to middle line.

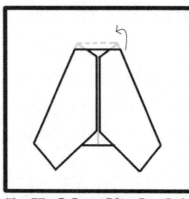

5. Fold a little bit of the top down away from you.

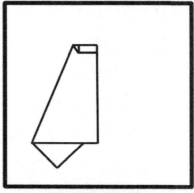

6. Fold in half toward you.

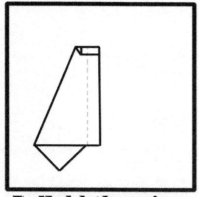

7. Fold the wing down on dotted line.

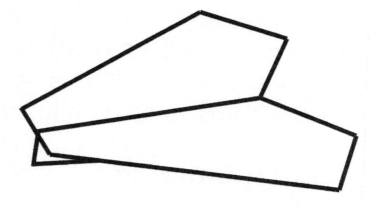

8. Fold the other wing down on the other side.

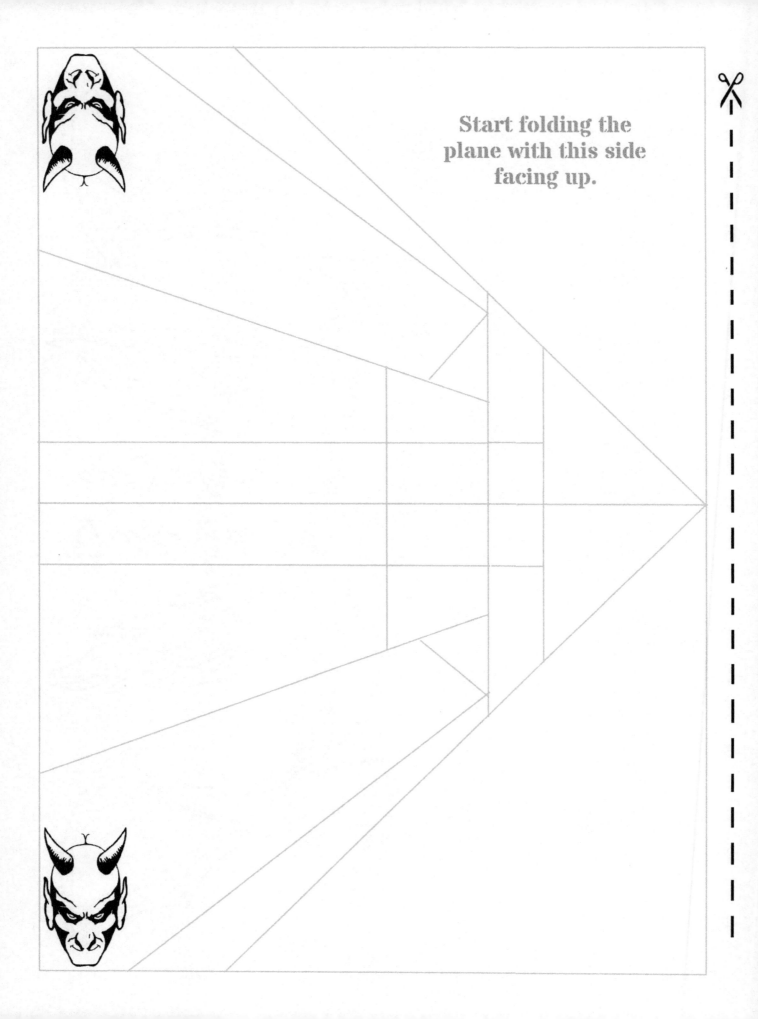

Start folding the
plane with this side
facing up.

DRILL BIT

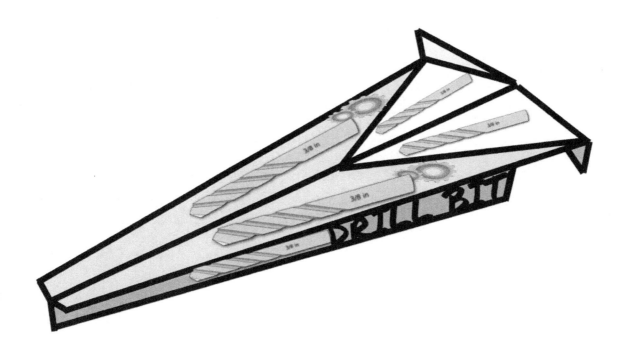

FF-DB102

TOP SECRET FILE

Name: Drill Bit

Drill Bit is quite a unique aircraft in that it was designed and built from spare parts of other jet planes. However, even though it is referred to as "flying junk", there is no mistaking its maneuverability and strike force as it has the ability to basically spin through the sky and also drill through hard surfaces such as other planes, hence its name "Drill Bit".

Superpower: Drill Bit's power is the ability to spin clockwise and counter-clockwise at very high speeds while at the same time flying forward and can basically drill a hole straight through an enemy invader.

STATS

- Top speed: While not in spin mode, Drill Bit can reach speeds up to Mach 2, however in spin mode this aircraft's speed is twice that.
- Agility: Drill Bit was designed for one thing and one thing only, to spin and fly straight. Although it does have the ability to turn in all directions, it is not its strong point.
- Stealth: This aircraft is not safe from enemy radar detectors unless it is in full spin mode.
- Armament: In case of spin mode malfunction, this aircraft is equipped with extra spare parts and tools that are used to propel toward enemy aircraft in order to render said aircraft incapacitated.

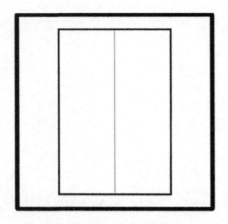

1. Fold the paper in half and open again.

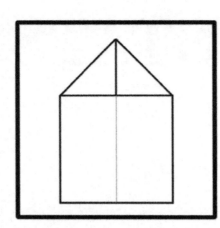

2. Fold top corners to the center.

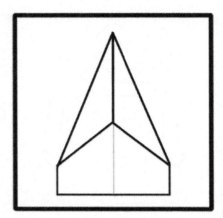

3. Fold side corners to the center.

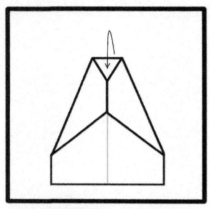

4. Fold the center nose toward you and flatten.

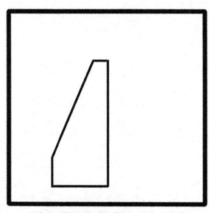

5. Fold in half toward you.

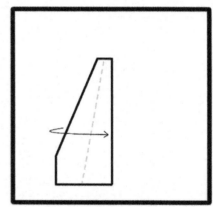

6. Fold the wings down on dotted line.

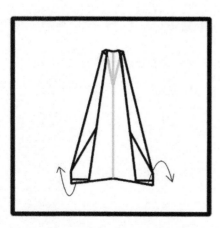

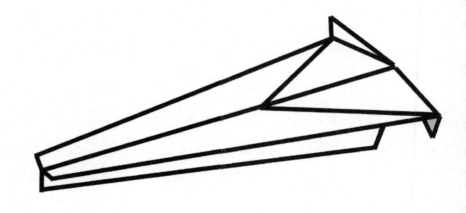

7. Fold one back wing flap up, fold the other one down.

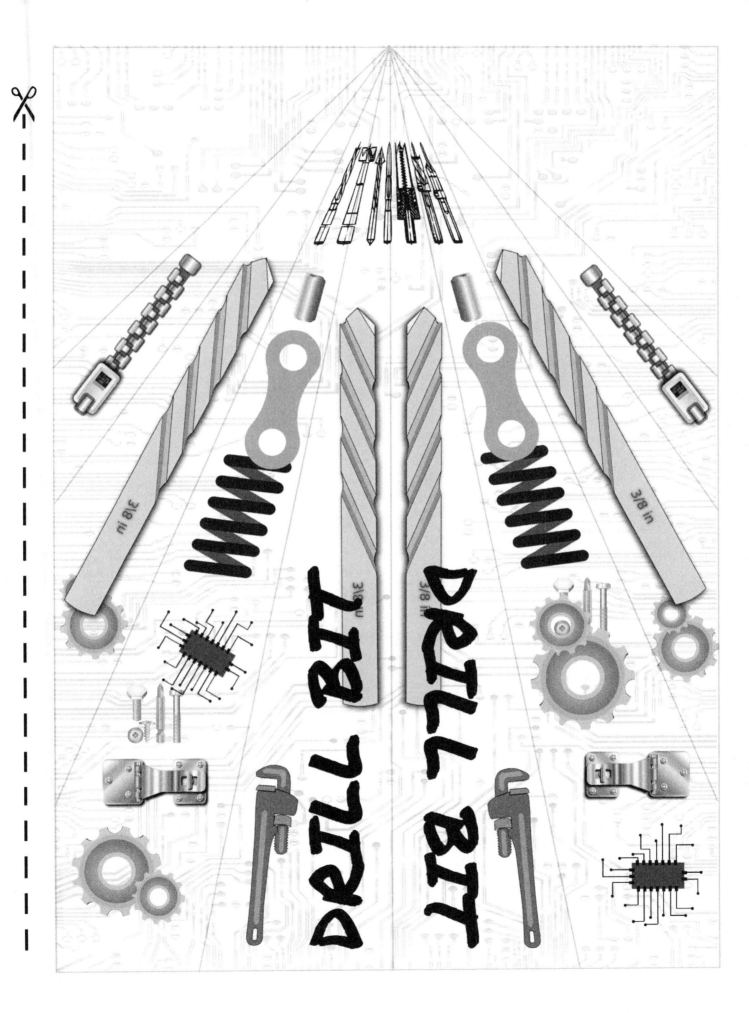

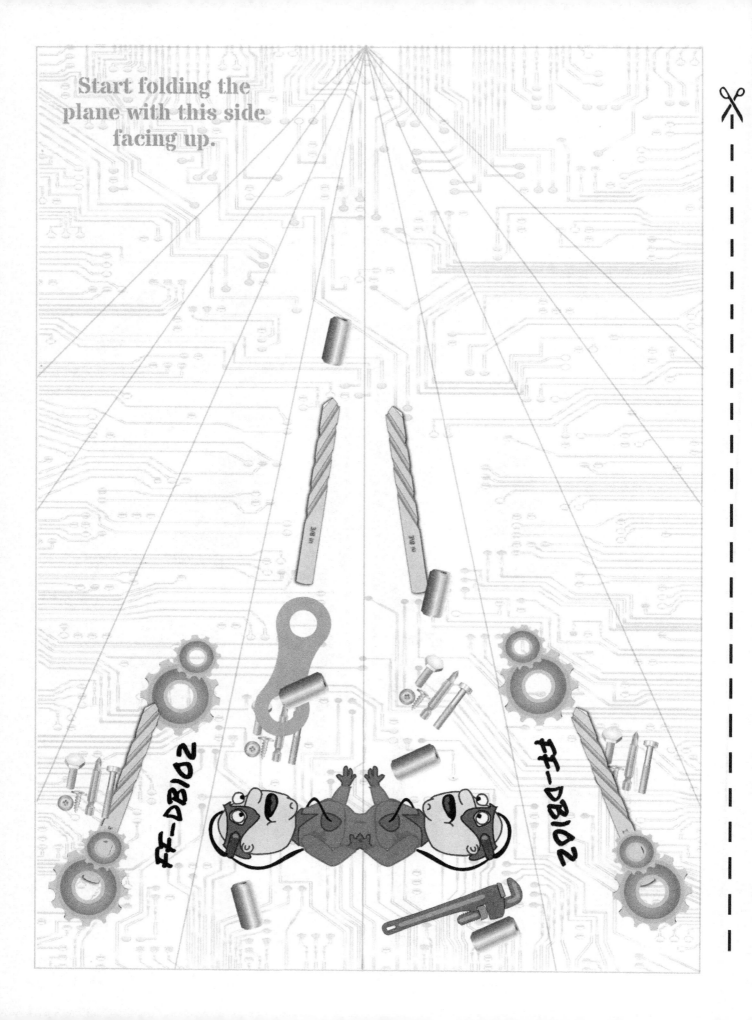

LOOPY
LEOPARD

FF-LL562

TOP SECRET FILE

Name: Loopy Leopard

This aircraft was designed to fool enemy planes. A top team of designers and engineers designed Loopy Leopard with nitro-injected hydraulics which allows this plane to change direction with its wing flaps very quickly causing the plane to do a complete 180-degree loop in mid-air. The designers also added camouflage to the fuselage mimicking that of a white leopard that hides this plane amongst the clouds from enemy sight.

Superpower: Loopy Leopard can suddenly disappear from the enemy's sights while being chased, completing a loop and then chase the enemy plane. Thus the hunted becomes the hunter.

STATS

- Top speed: While flying straight, Loopy Leopard does not fly very fast, however when on the downturn of its famous loop it can reach speeds up to Mach 4.
- Agility: This aircraft although not swift on horizontal turning, is however very fast at the vertical climb and the vertical descent.
- Stealth: Loopy Leopard is so fast when entering and exiting its loop, that to enemy planes it may seem to have disappeared in front of their eyes, only to reappear at their tail. When not in loop mode this aircraft is covered in white and gray leopard spots making it hard to see in clouds.
- Armament: The aircraft is equipped with a reinforced titanium and molybdenum-plated nose for ramming into enemy planes.

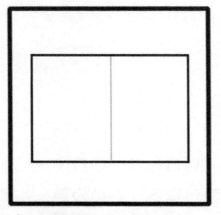

1. Fold paper in half the long way and open again.

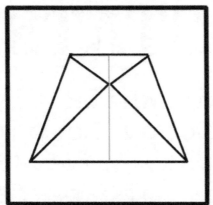

2. Fold left & right corners to center line.

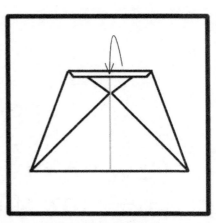

3. Fold top down toward you just a little bit.

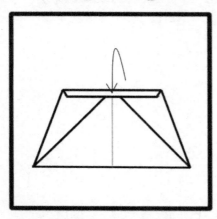

4. Fold top down again three more times.

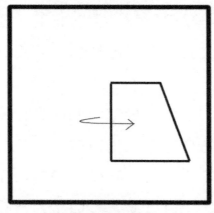

5. Fold in half toward you.

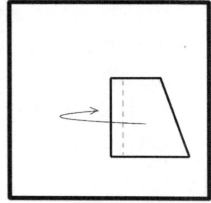

6. Fold wings down on dotted line.

7. Fold wing tips up. Cut slits to make flap at back of wings.

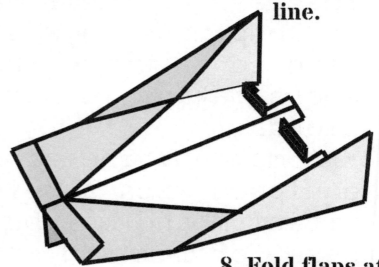

8. Fold flaps at back up.

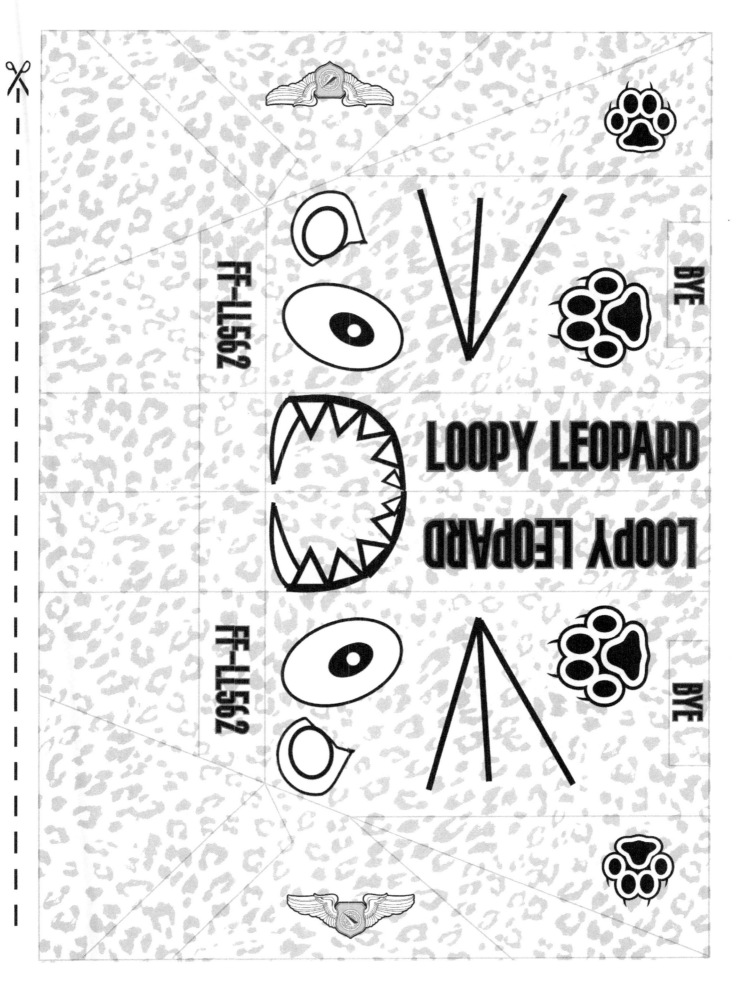

Start folding the plane with this side facing up.

IRON NINJA

FF-IN222

TOP SECRET FILE

Name: Iron Ninja

As its name suggests this aircraft was designed with two things in mind, strength, and stealth. Iron Ninja is the perfect fighter plane to sneak up on an enemy without the pilot or ground control even knowing where it came from. This plane is clad in a lightweight but super strong iron alloy shell making it very fast but also able to withstand anything that is thrown at it.

Superpower: Iron Ninja is covered in a special iron alloy that can refract light becoming chameleon-like to blend into any background making it virtually invisible to the naked eye. The design of this unique iron skin is highly classified.

STATS

- Top speed: Iron Ninja is extremely light with a very powerful jet engine allowing it to reach speeds of up to Mach 5.
- Agility: Because of its lightweight and size this aircraft displays amazing acrobatic ability able to turn left, right, up, and down in milliseconds.
- Stealth: Iron Ninja was designed with stealth in mind. Just like the name suggests, this plane, with its highly classified outer shell, can appear and disappear at will confusing the enemy and ultimately defeating them with a surprise attack.
- Armament: The aircraft is equipped with titanium-plated throwing stars which can render an enemy plane immobile in seconds.

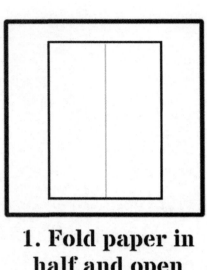

1. Fold paper in half and open again.

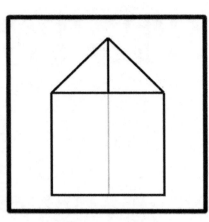

2. Fold the top corners down to center.

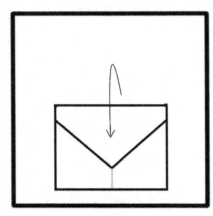

3. Fold the top center point down to look like an envelope.

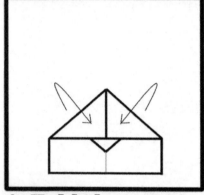

4. Fold the corners to center leaving a little triangle at bottom.

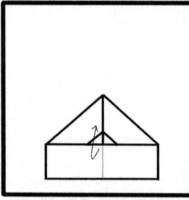

5. Fold the little triangle up.

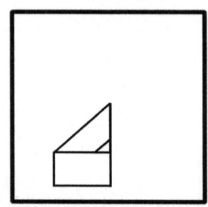

6. Fold in half away from you.

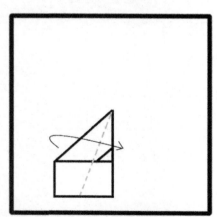

7. Fold wing down on dotted line.

8. Fold the second wing down.

IRON
NINJA

NINJA
IRON

FF-IN222

FF-IN222

HASHTAG HURRICANE

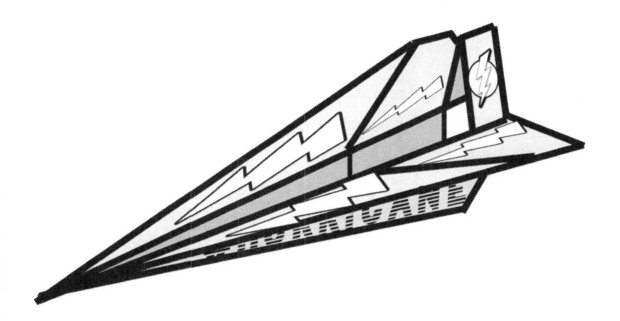

FF-HH002

TOP SECRET FILE

Name: Hashtag Hurricane

Originally designed as a vehicle to promote military propaganda, Hashtag Hurricane has since been retrofitted with laser technology that has the ability to zap an enemy plane out of the sky. The body was also designed with a rear tail keeping it stable in a high-wind situation such as a hurricane and/or tornado.

Superpower: This aircraft's superpower is the ability to keep a consistent speed in high winds without the fuselage being ripped to shreds as is the case of normal fighter aircraft.

STATS

- Top speed: While at cruising speed Hashtag Hurricane has a top speed of Mach 2, however when flying through strong winds it has a top speed of Mach 4.
- Agility: Built with a tail at its rear, this aircraft has the ability to remain stable in high-wind situations allowing for incredible agility.
- Stealth: While not that stealthy outside of high-wind situations such as a hurricane or tornado this aircraft can become virtually invisible in a wind storm because of its high speed.
- Armament: Hashtag Hurricane is equipped with two gamma-ray lasers which it can use to protect itself from enemy attacks.

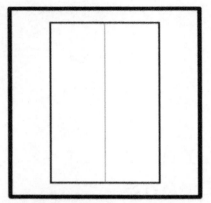

1. Fold paper in half and open again.

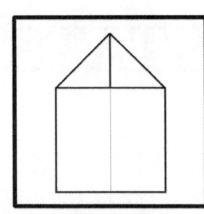

2. Fold top corners toward center line.

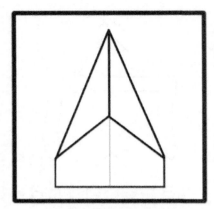

3. Fold side corners to the center line.

4. Fold in half.

5. Fold the wings down the dotted line on both sides.

6. Make one cut at back, up to the wing fold.

7. Push up to make tail.

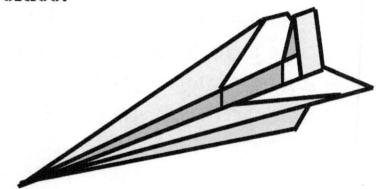

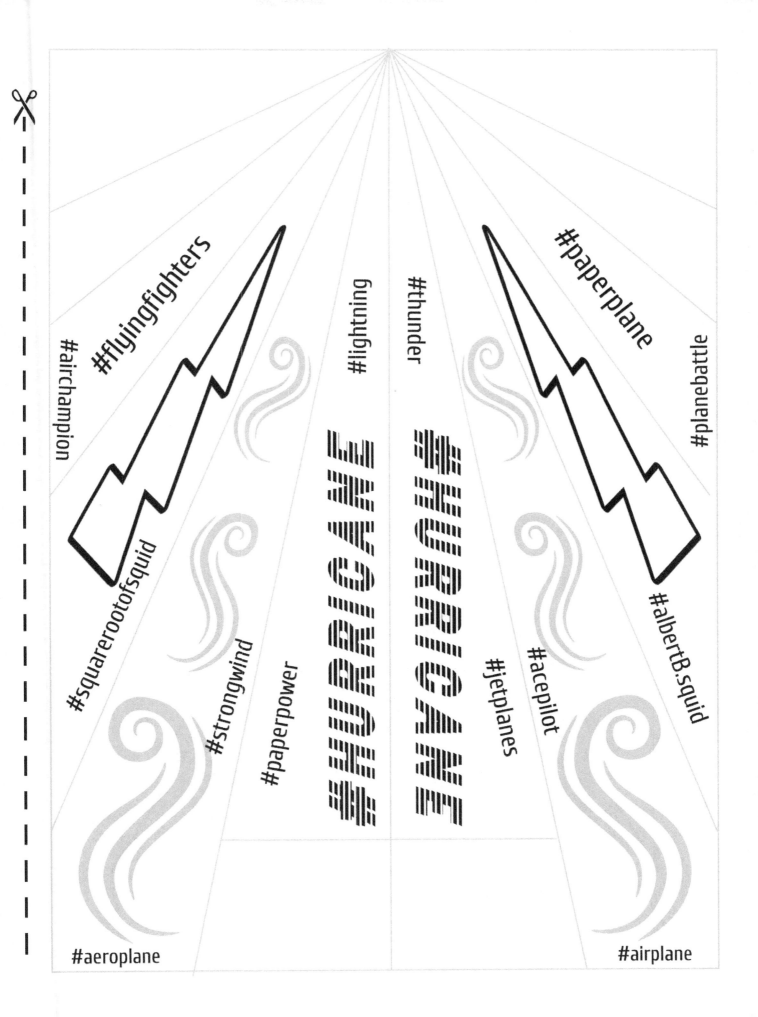

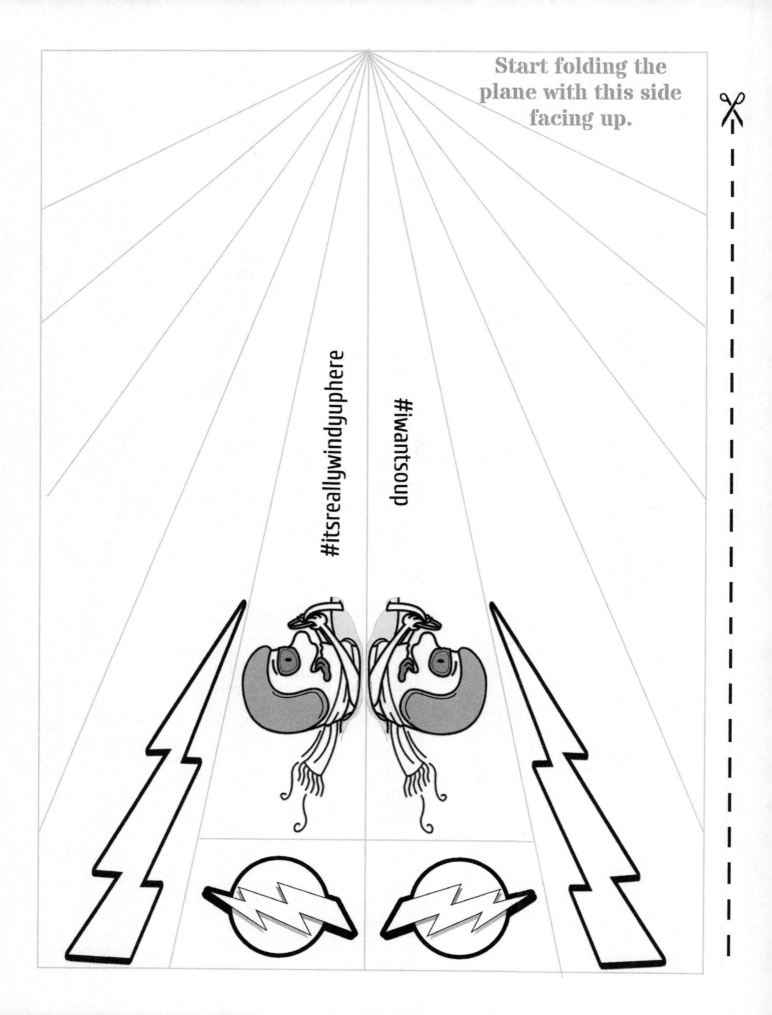

Start folding the plane with this side facing up.

#itsreallywindyuphere

#iwantsoup

KID SQUID

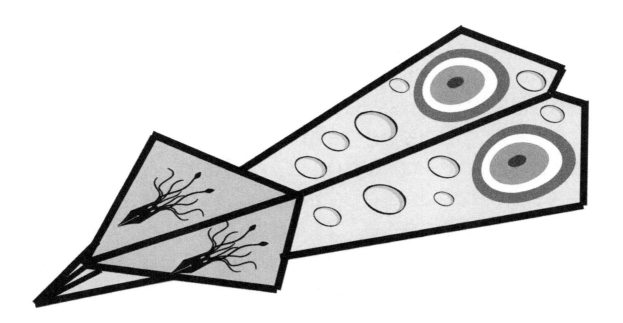

FF-DD662

TOP SECRET FILE

Name: Kid Squid

This aircraft was designed to be an enemy threat to not only planes in the sky but also military boats and submarines in the sea. Kid Squid's highly pressurized interior allows it to fly into space and also to the bottom of the ocean making for an awesome all-around aircraft to fight enemy attacks on any playing field.

Superpower: Just like its aquatic equivalent, Kid Squid can shoot a substance very similar to black ink to make a quick escape by blinding an enemy aircraft and disappearing into thin air.

STATS

- Top speed: Kid Squid can maintain a speed of up to Mach 3 in the air. As for the water, it can get up to 300 knots above the surface and 150 knots below the surface.
- Agility: Because of the extra front wings, this aircraft can maneuver quite well in the air and in the sea.
- Stealth: Kid Squid was designed for stealth. With its oil-based black ink projectile superpower it is virtually impossible to spot by enemy aircraft once the ink is projected into the air or water.
- Armament: Along with its oil-based ink wells and ink propulsion docks, Kid Squid is also armed with multi-jointed robotic arms that act like tentacles to grab enemy aircraft, boats, or submarines out of the air or water.

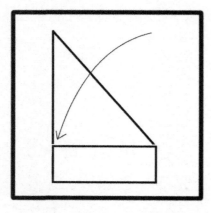

1. Fold top right corner down.

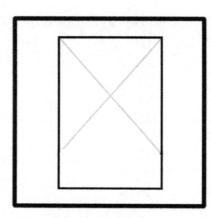

2. Fold top left corner down. Re-open to make an "x".

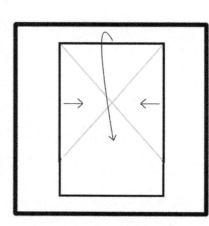

3. Push the two sides together and fold down top to make a triangle.

4. Fold these two corners up to center.

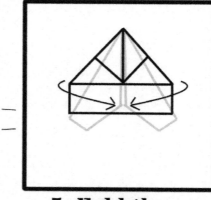

5. Fold these corners to center line but under top triangle.

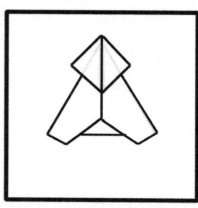

6. It should look like this at this point.

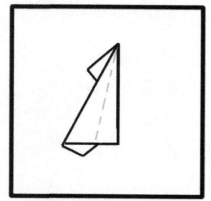

8. Fold down front wings.

7. Fold the wing down along the dotted line on both sides.

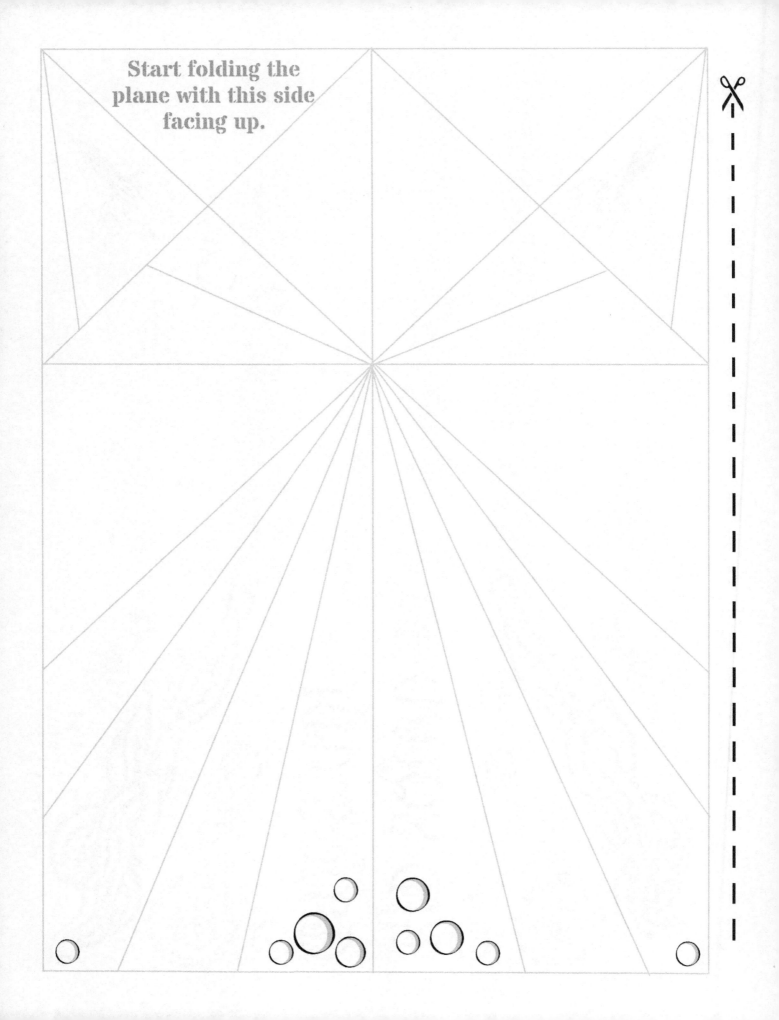

Start folding the
plane with this side
facing up.

M.O.M.
(MONSTER OF MAYHEM)

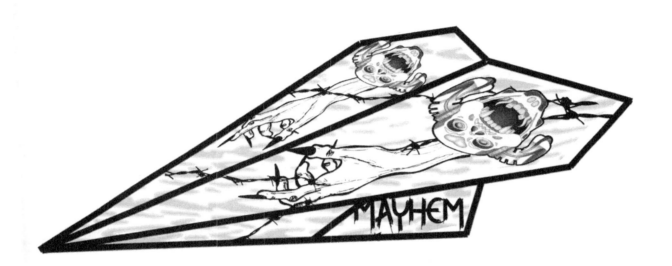

FF-MM772

TOP SECRET FILE

Name: M.O.M. (Monster of Mayhem)

This aircraft, Monster of Mayhem abbreviated as M.O.M., has been correctly named, as it wreaks havoc on its enemies creating chaos. It is the meanest plane in the sky hands down. Designed with the latest advanced technology such as the newly developed neural computer system that knows what the enemy is thinking before they do, plus a super-sharp spiky exterior, this plane is pure evil in the sky.

Superpower: This aircraft's specialty is reading the minds of enemy pilots. By knowing their every move it can plan and take action with its merciless attack in seconds.

STATS

- Top speed: Not only is M.O.M. a ruthless opponent it is also the fastest plane out there today reaching speeds upwards of Mach 7 being unrivaled by any other plane when it comes to speed.
- Agility: With this aircraft's compact size and larger-than-average wing span, maneuvering in every direction very quickly is a piece of cake.
- Stealth: Equipped with an advanced neural computer that knows what the enemy is thinking, M.O.M. can stay off of enemy radar very easily and will not be seen coming until it's too late.
- Armament: Aside from the super-advanced neural computer, this aircraft is also equipped with steel monster claws that can reach out and crush an enemy plane like a tin can.

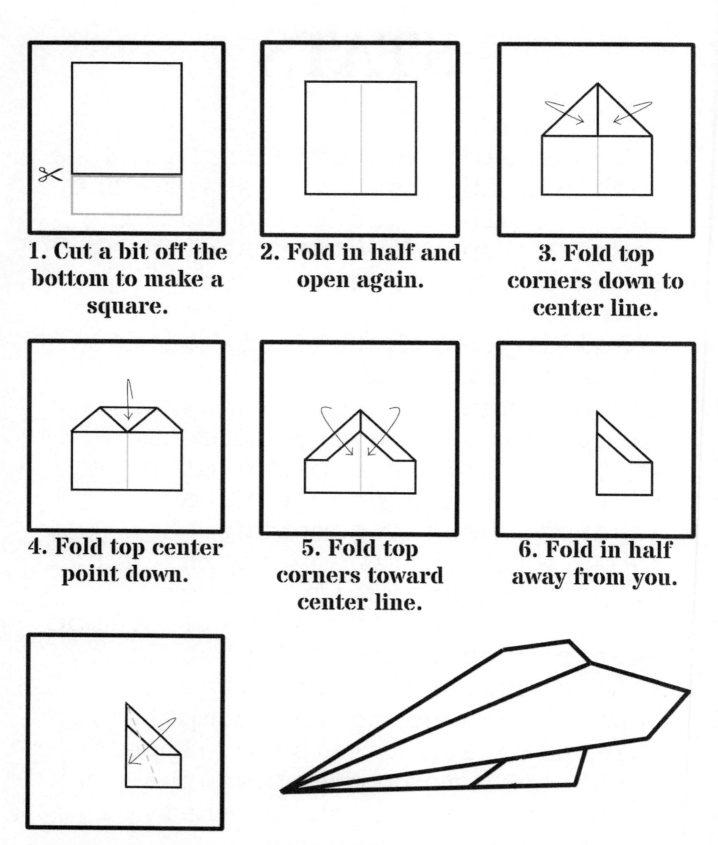

1. Cut a bit off the bottom to make a square.

2. Fold in half and open again.

3. Fold top corners down to center line.

4. Fold top center point down.

5. Fold top corners toward center line.

6. Fold in half away from you.

7. Fold wings down on the diagonal dotted line on both sides.

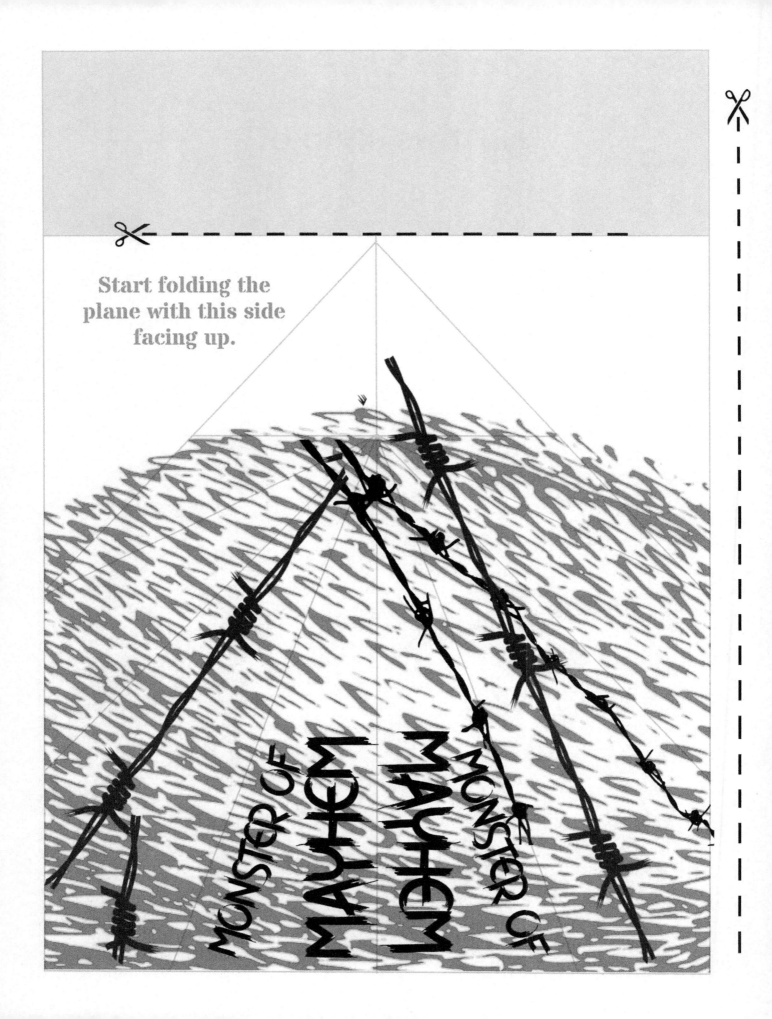

Start folding the plane with this side facing up.

DESIGN YOUR OWN
PLANES

Hello pilot! On the following pages are some plans for you to draw on and make your own fighter planes. Each one of the templates has its own code. This code will let you know exactly where to put things on your plane before it is folded. Come up with some innovative ideas then draw and color the designs, cut them out, and fold them according to the same directions from the other planes in this book. Then you are ready for BATTLE! Have a great mission pilot!

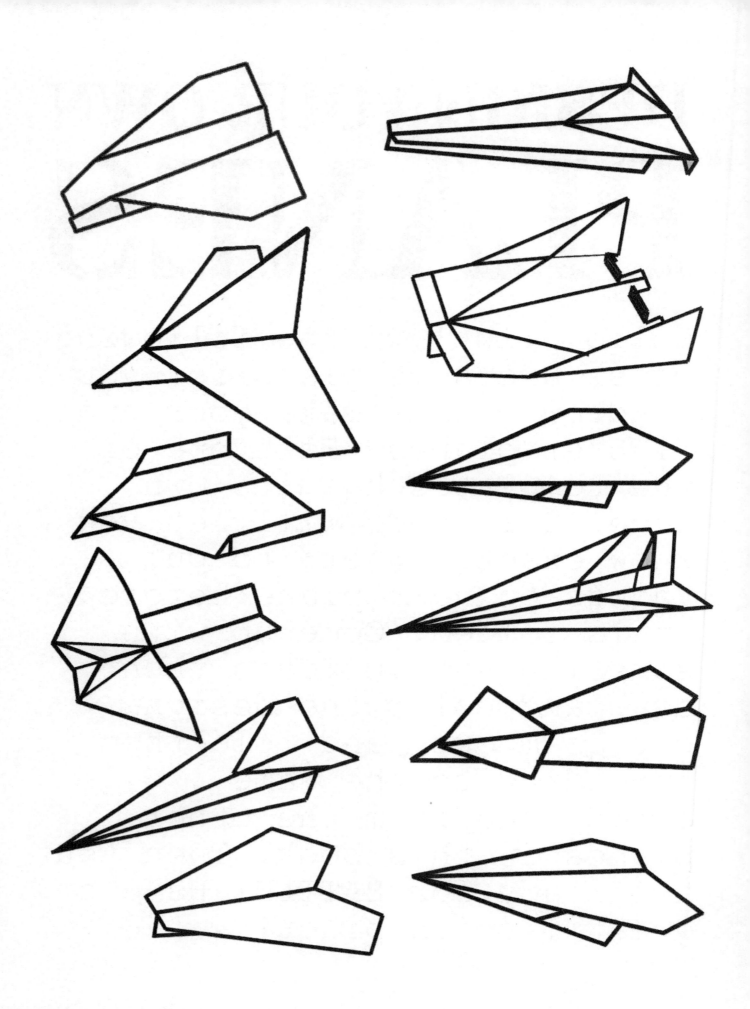

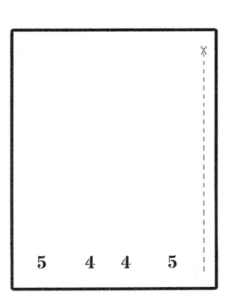

PLANE 1

1. Outer Side
2. Bottom Wing
3. Top Wing Front
4. Inner Side
5. Top Wing Back

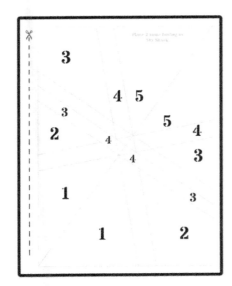
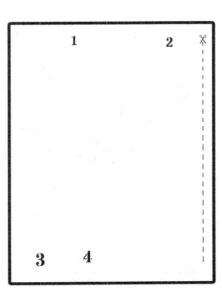

PLANE 2

1. Fin
2. Top Wing
3. Bottom Wing
4. Outer Side
5. Inner Side

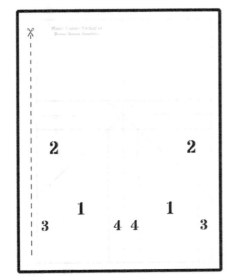
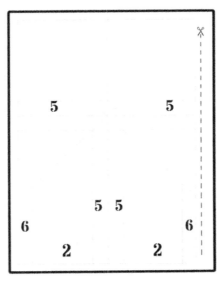

PLANE 3

1. Top Wing
2. Bottom Wing
3. Inner Wing Tip
4. Inner Side
5. Outer Side
6. Outer Wing Tip

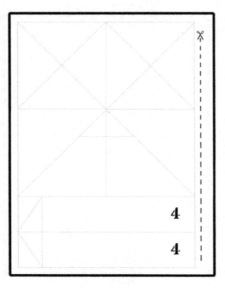

PLANE 4

1. Bottom Wing
2. Top Wing
3. Inner Tail
4. Outer Tail

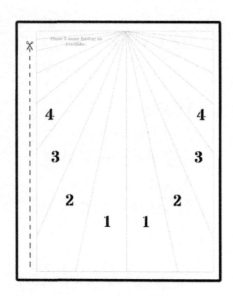
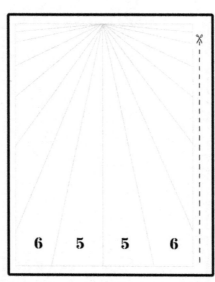

PLANE 5

1. Outer Side
2. Bottom Wing
3. Top Wing Front
4. Inner Front
5. Inner Back
6. Top Wing Back

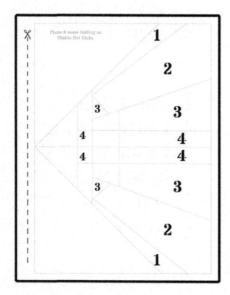
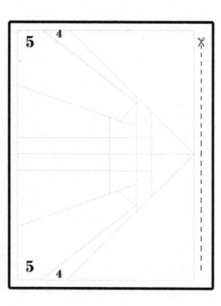

PLANE 6

1. Inner Side
2. Top Wing
3. Bottom Wing
4. Outer Side
5. Bottom Wing

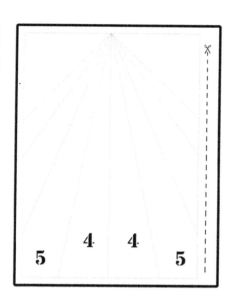

PLANE 7

1. Outer Side
2. Bottom Wing
3. Top Wing Front
4. Inner Side
5. Top Wing Back

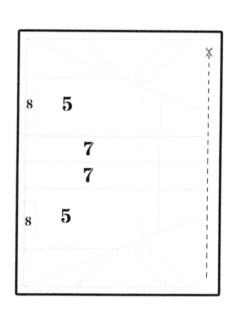

PLANE 8

1. Bottom Wing
2. Outer Side
3. Outer Wing Tip
4. Inner Wing Tip
5. Top Wing
6. Outer Back Flap
7. Inner Side
8. Inner Back Flap

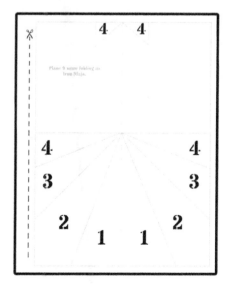
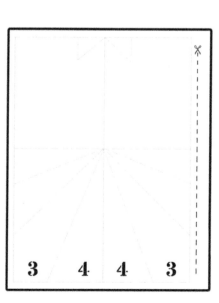

PLANE 9

1. Inner Side
2. Top Wing
3. Bottom Wing
4. Outer Side

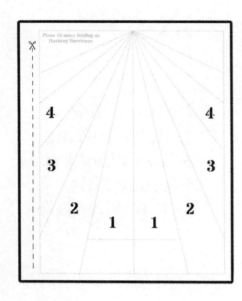
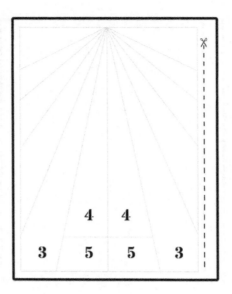

PLANE 10

1. Outer Side
2. Bottom Wing
3. Top Wing Front
4. Inner Side
5. Outer Tail

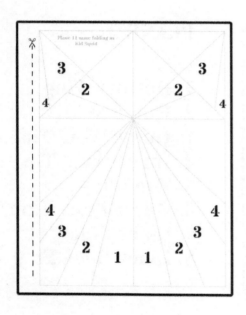
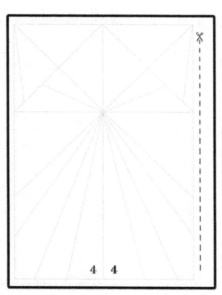

PLANE 11

1. Outer Side
2. Bottom Wing
3. Top Wing
4. Inner Side

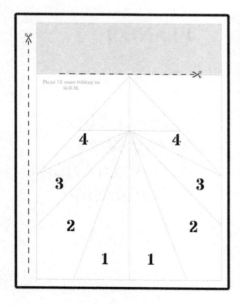
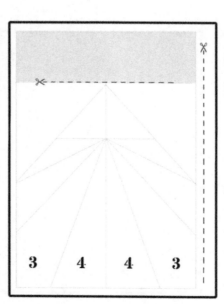

PLANE 12

1. Inner Side
2. Top Wing
3. Bottom Wing
4. Outer Side

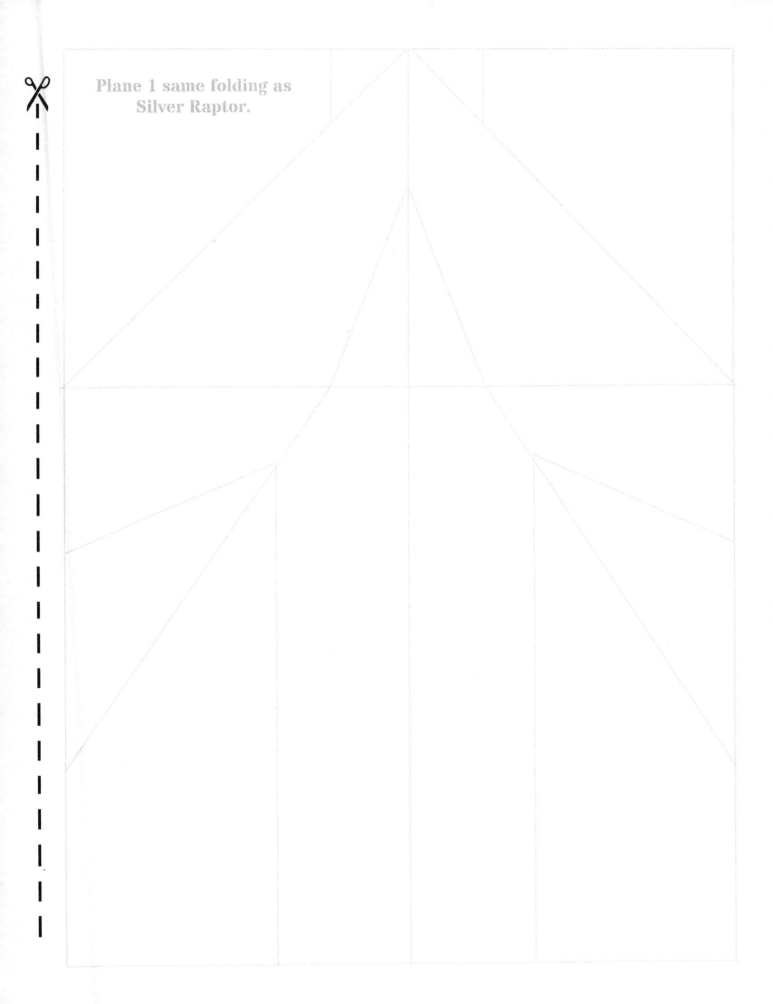

Plane 1 same folding as
Silver Raptor.

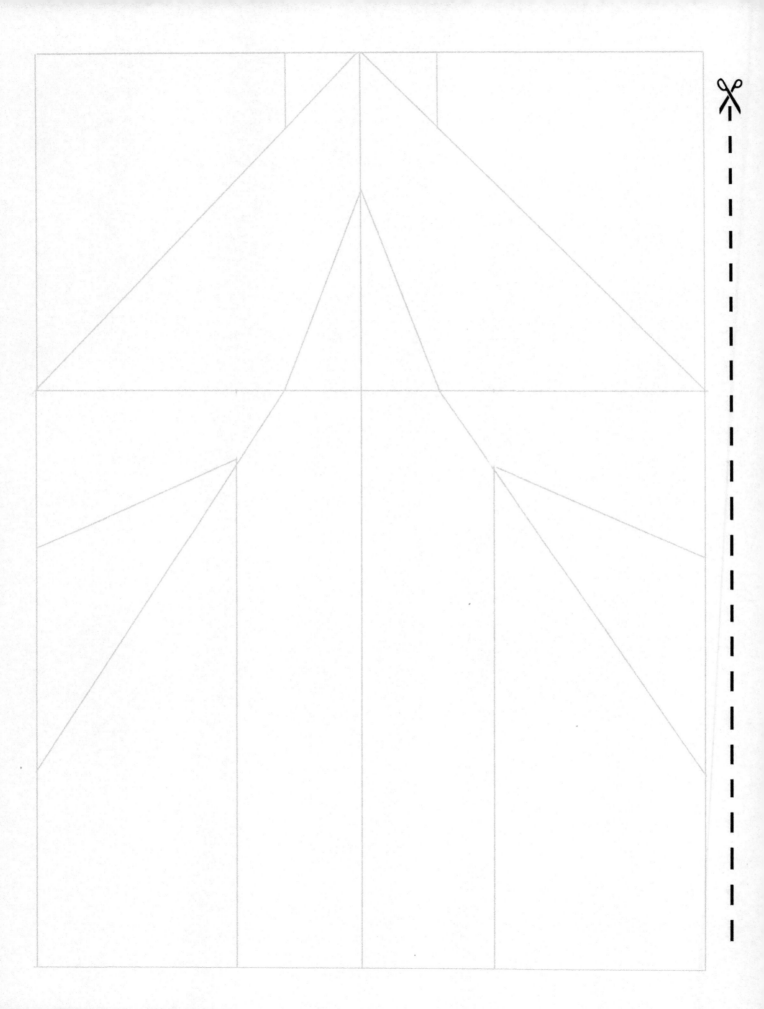

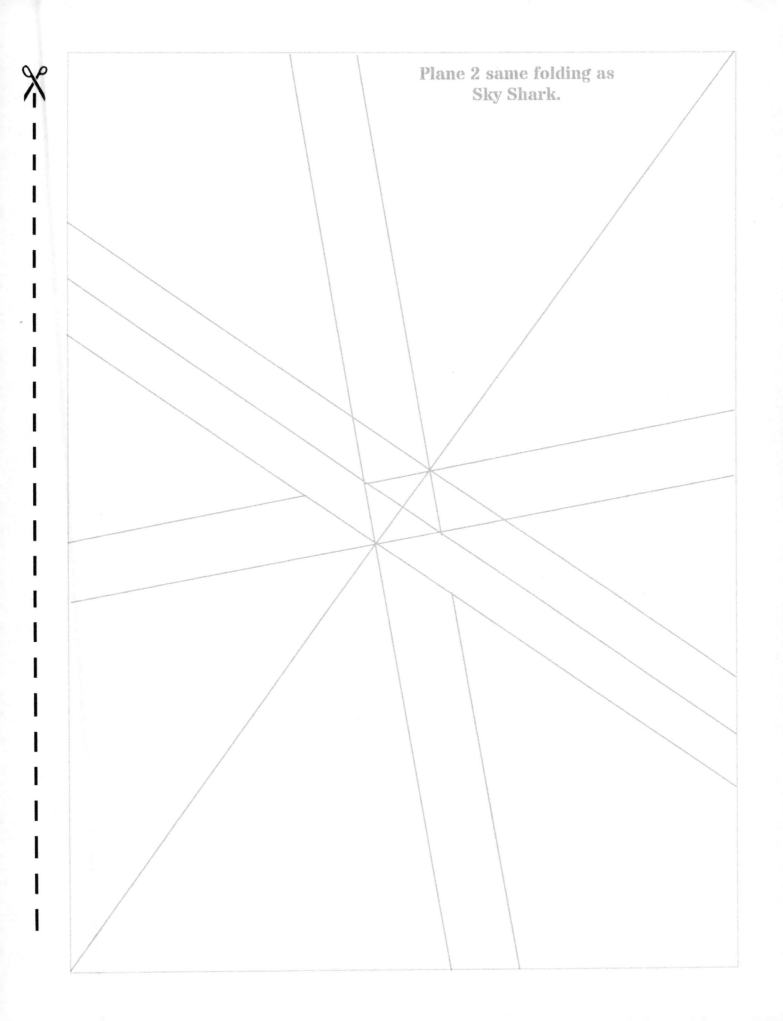

Plane 2 same folding as
Sky Shark.

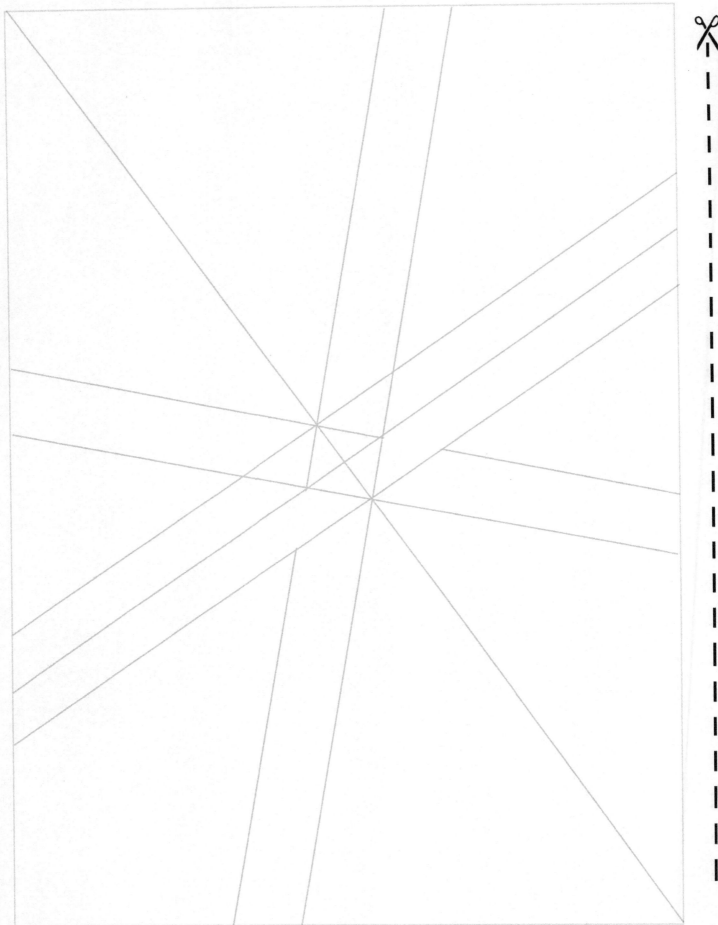

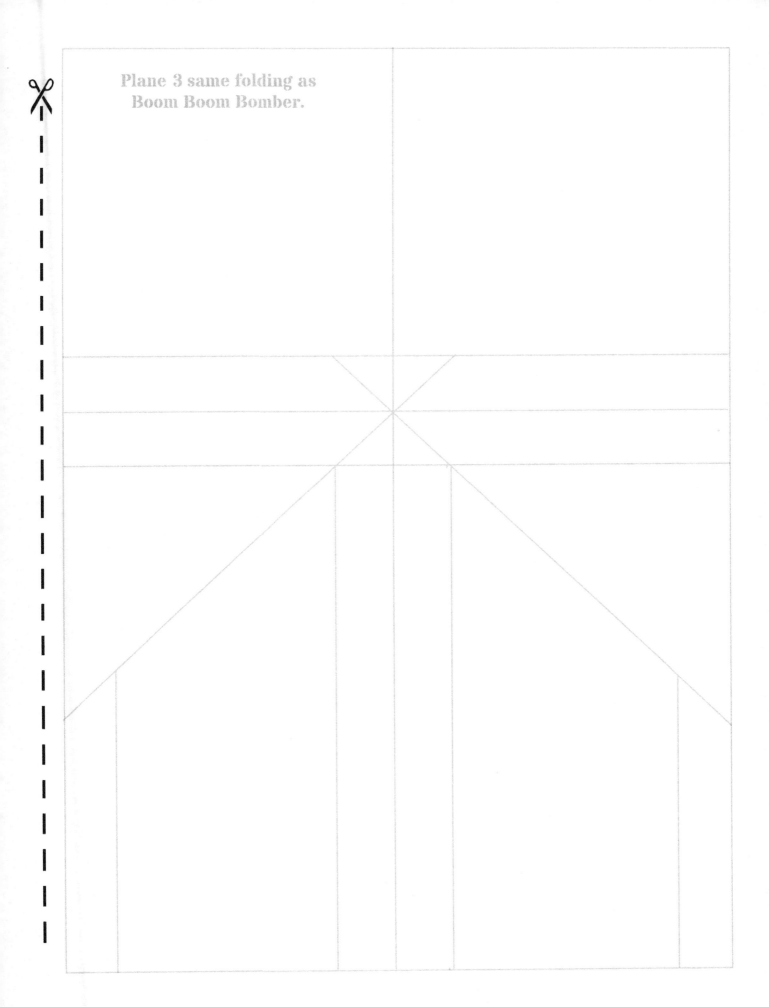

Plane 3 same folding as
Boom Boom Bomber.

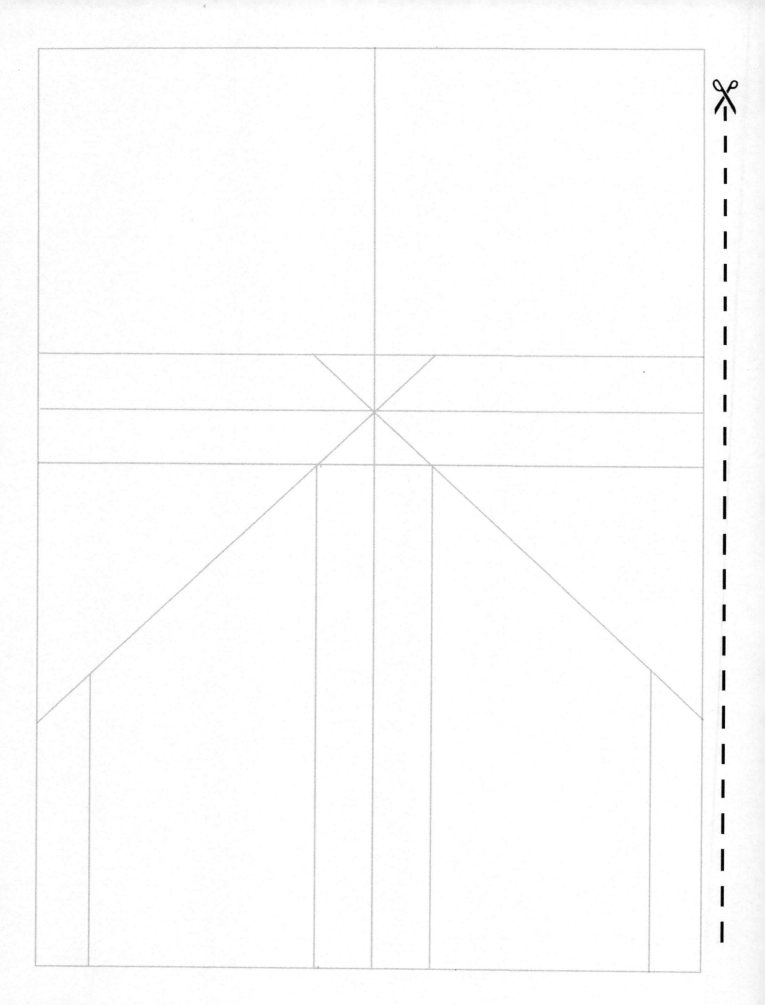

Plane 4 same folding as
Dragon Fire.

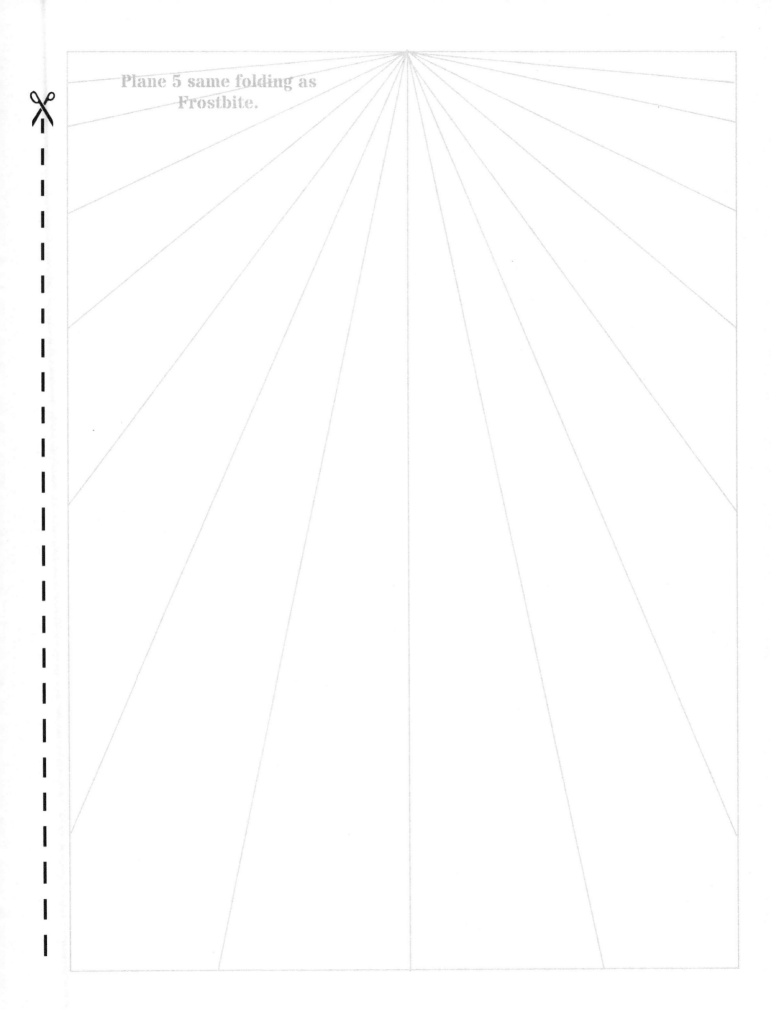

Plane 5 same folding as Frostbite.

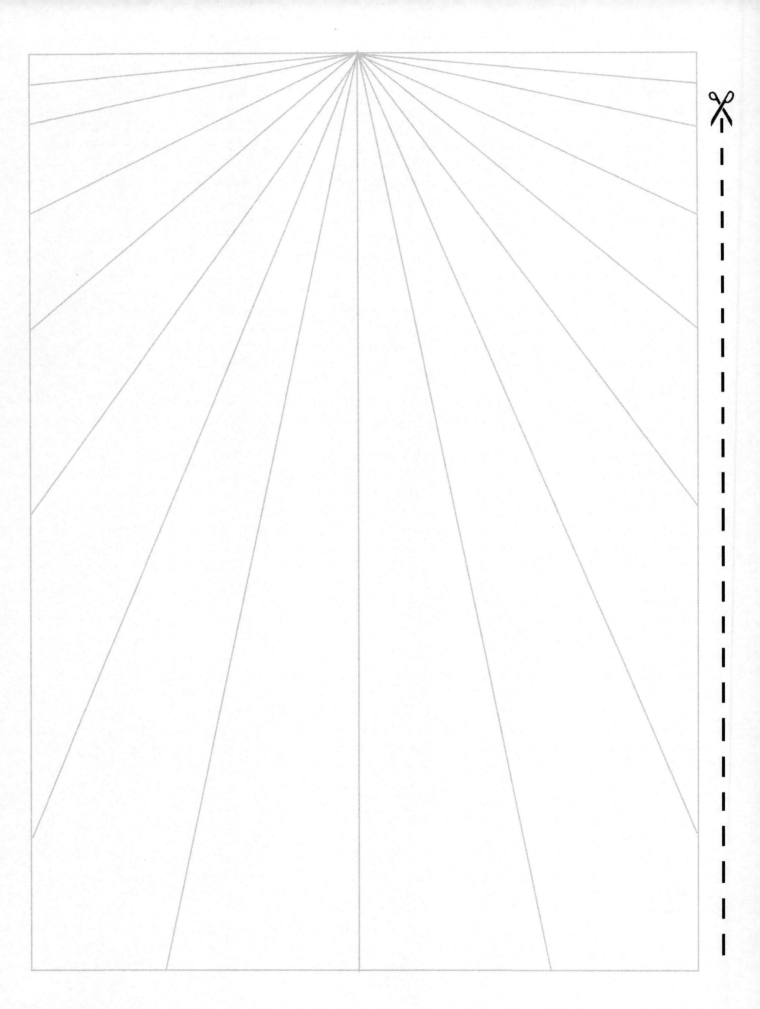

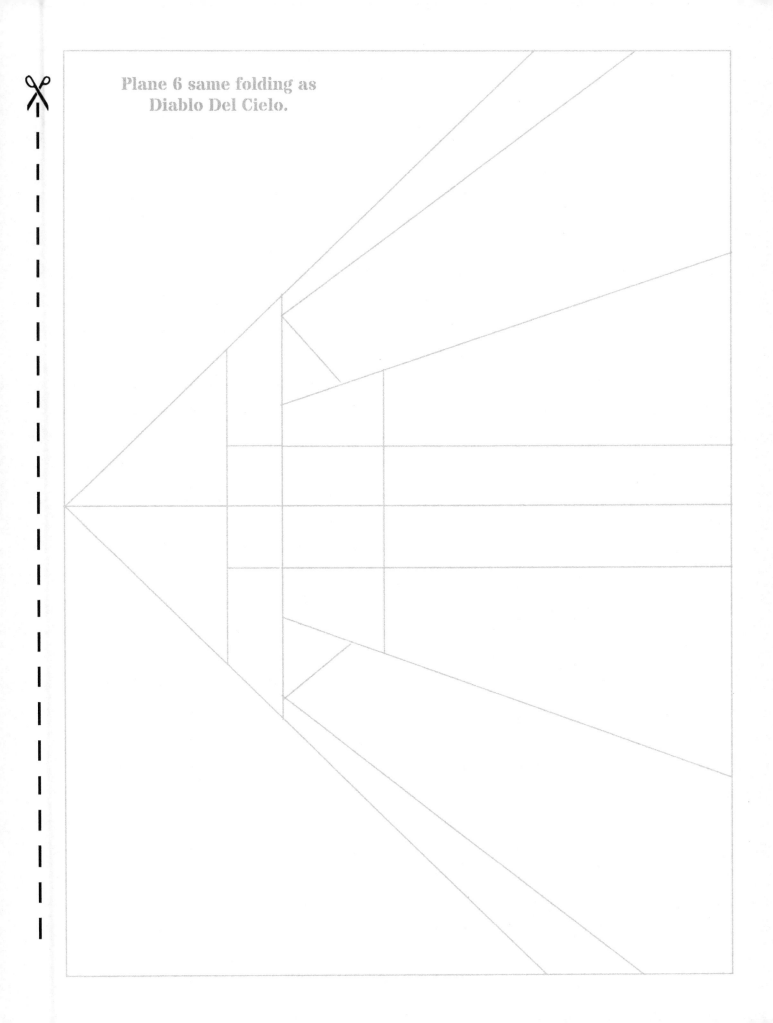

Plane 6 same folding as
Diablo Del Cielo.

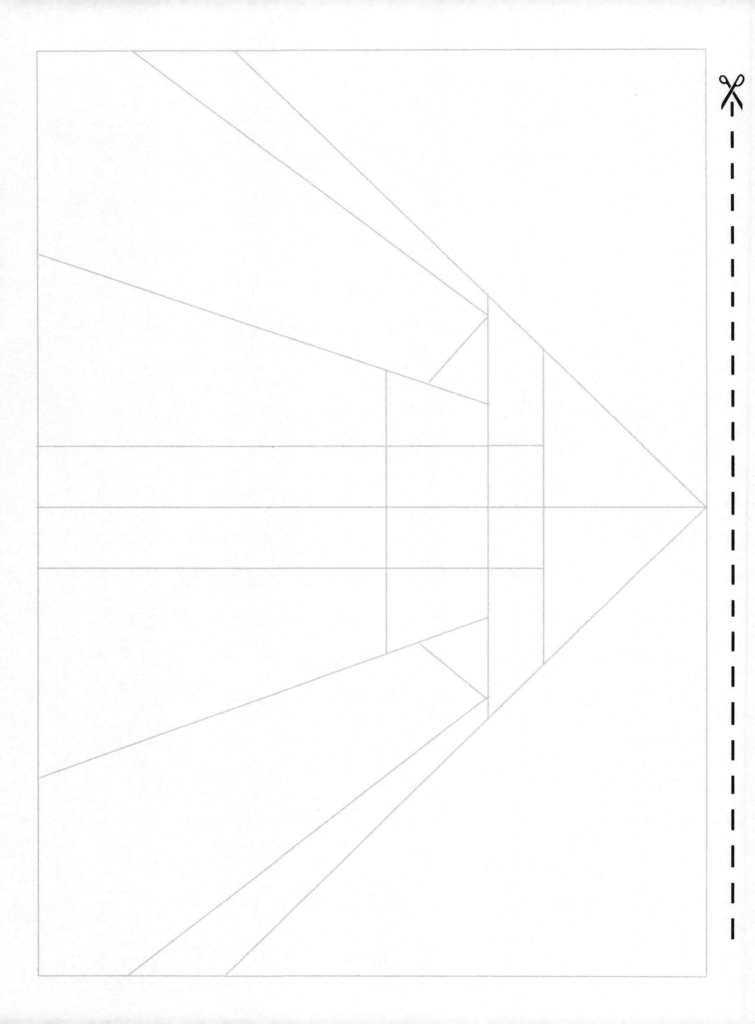

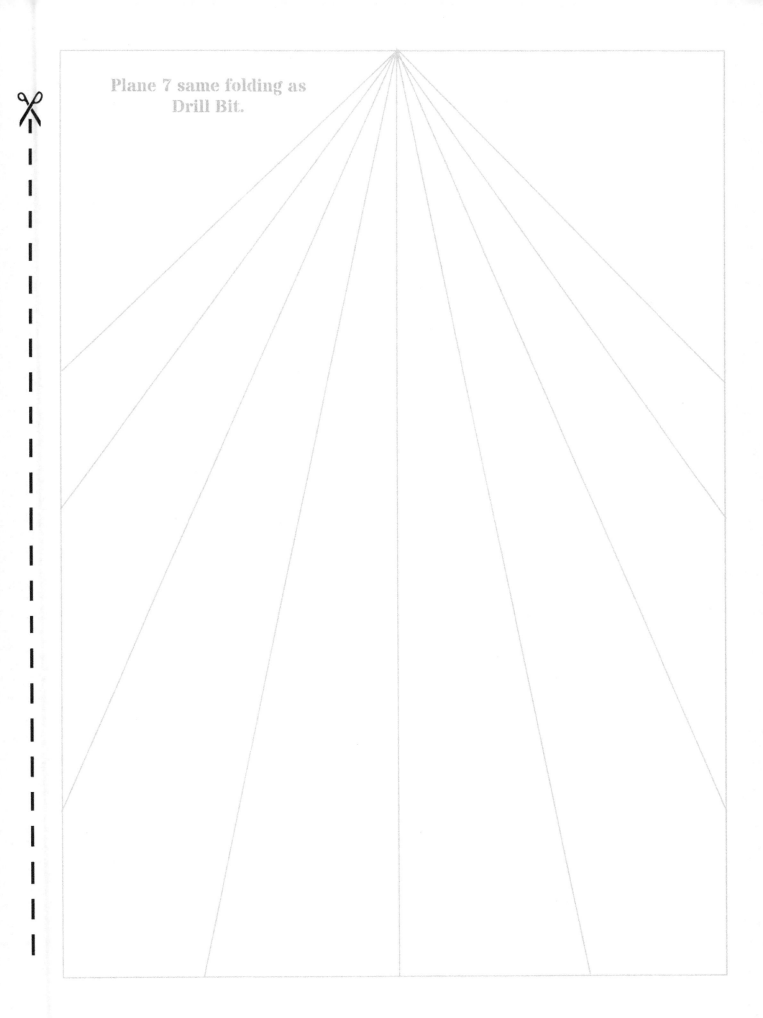

Plane 7 same folding as
Drill Bit.

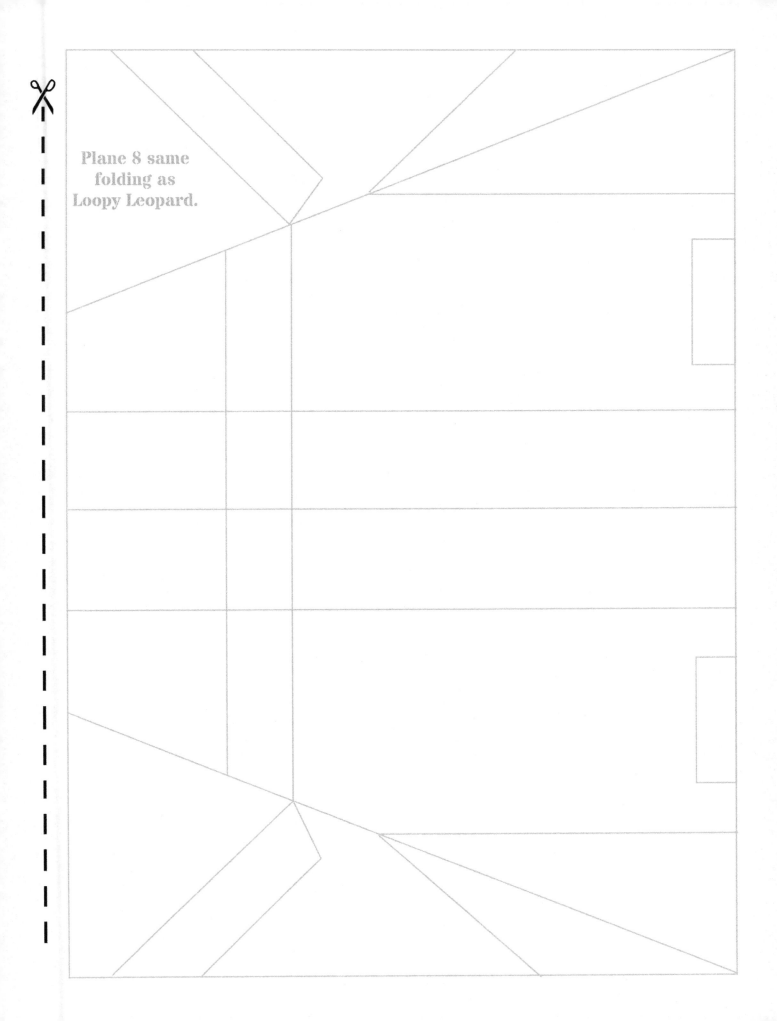

Plane 8 same
folding as
Loopy Leopard.

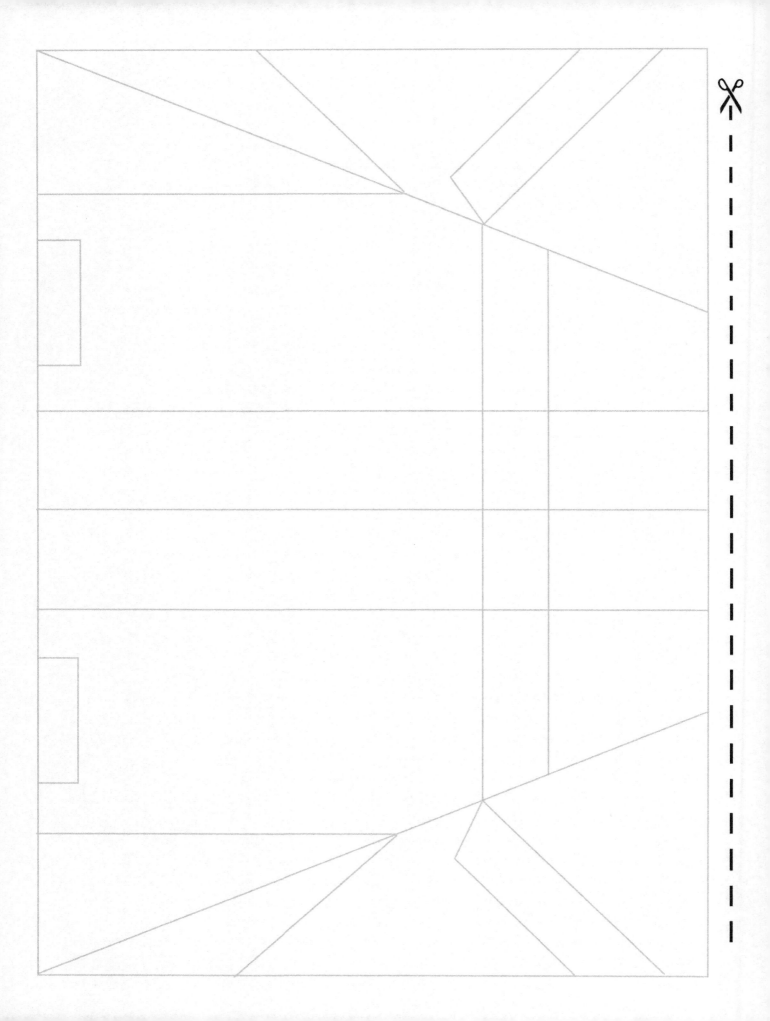

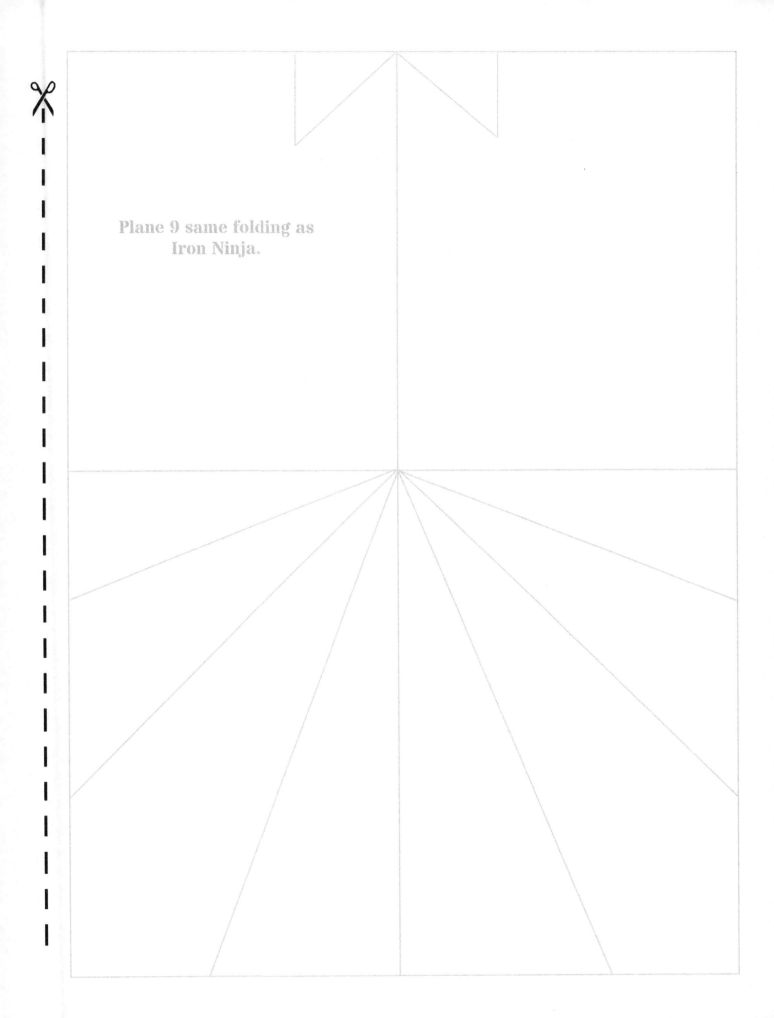

Plane 9 same folding as
Iron Ninja.

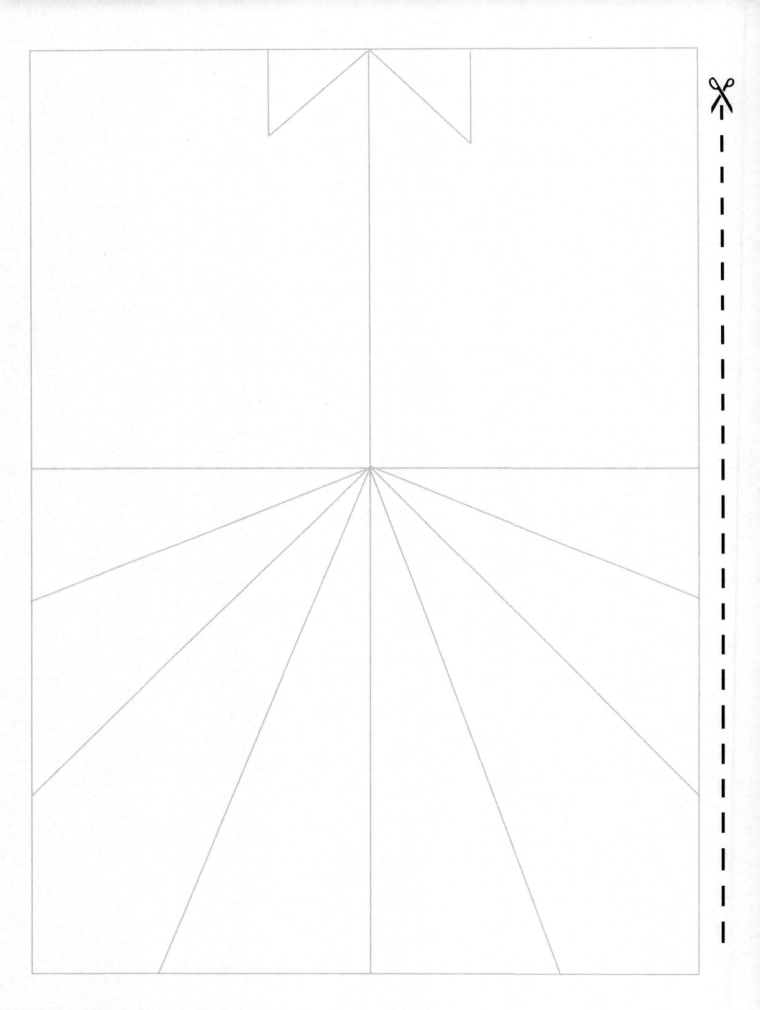

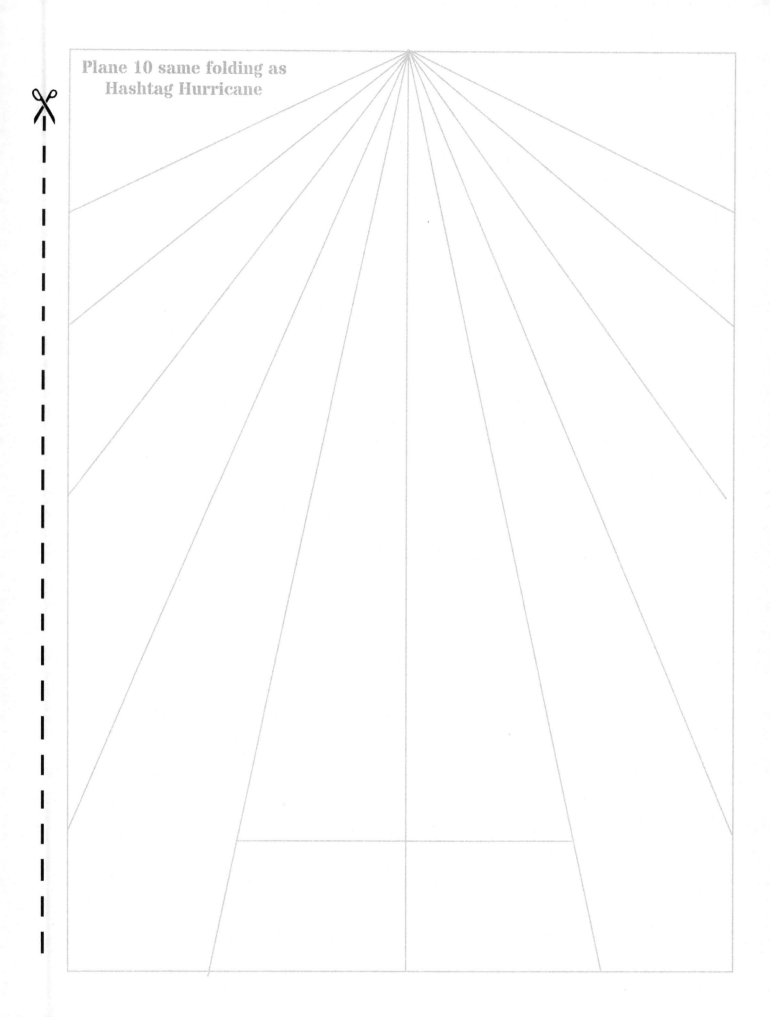

Plane 10 same folding as
Hashtag Hurricane

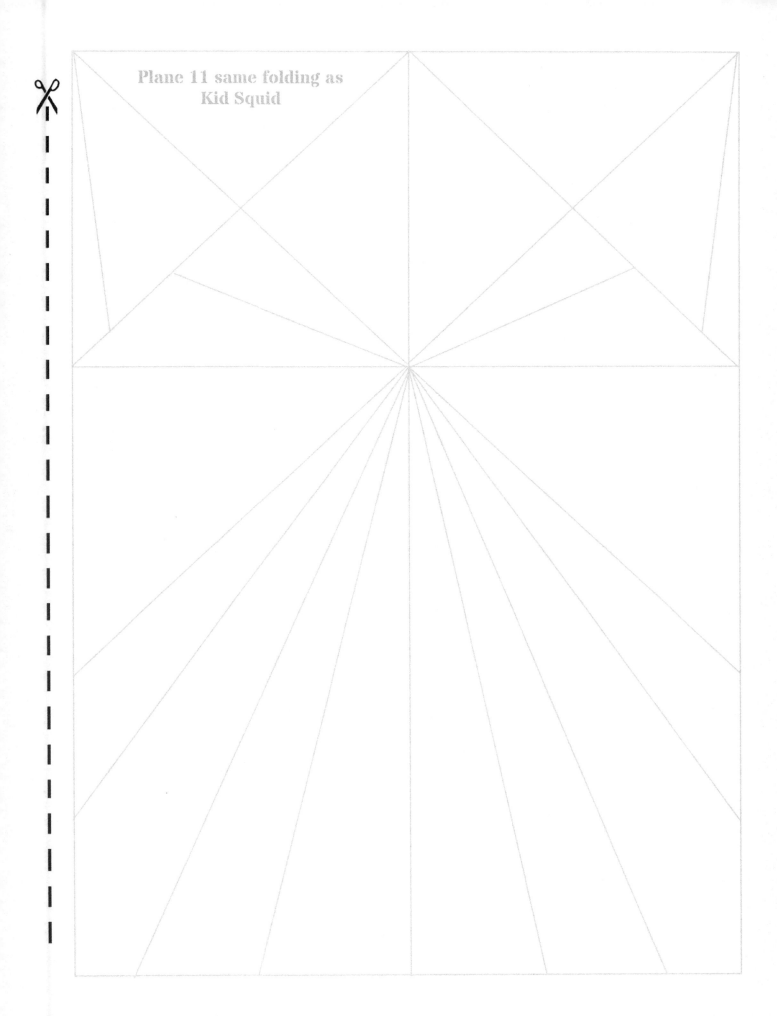

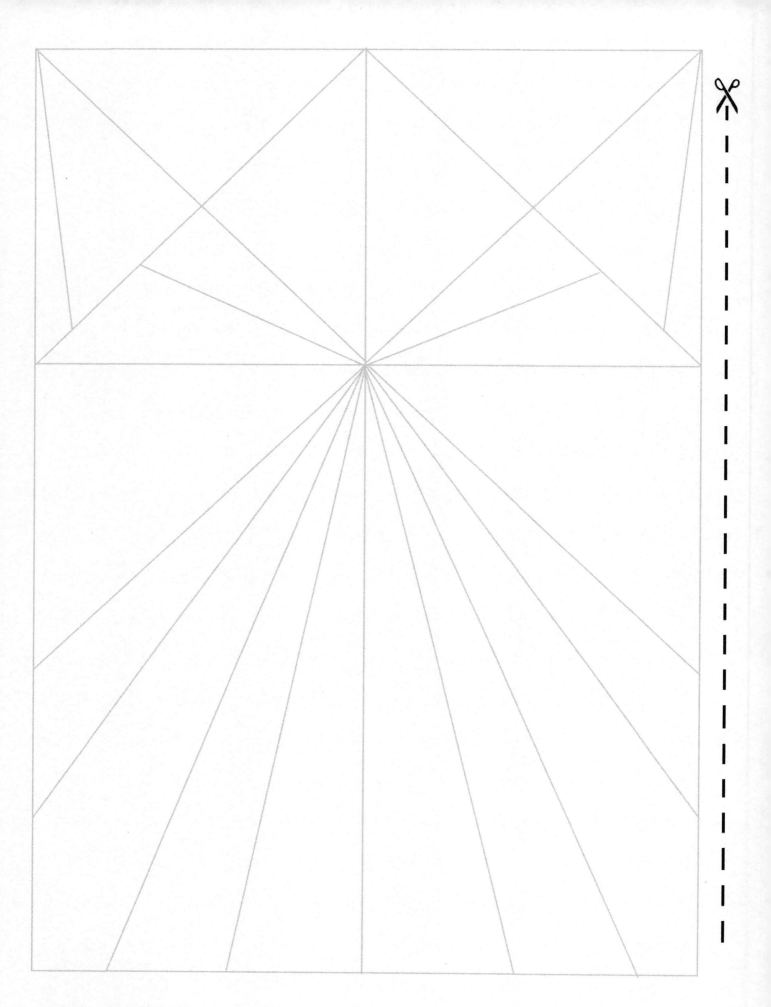

Plane 12 same folding as
M.O.M.

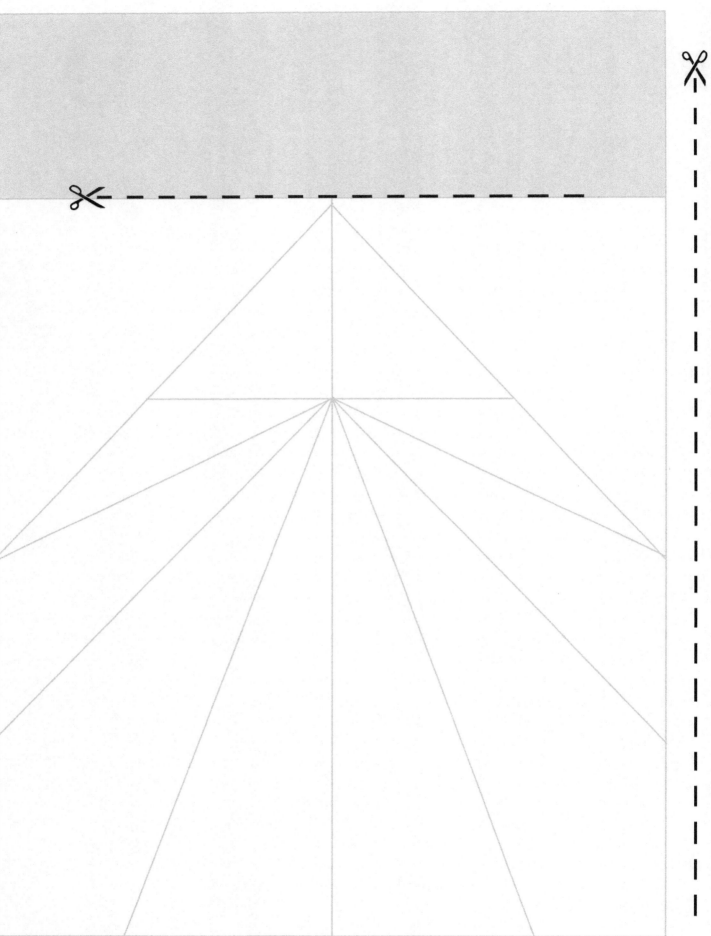

IT'S TIME TO BATTLE

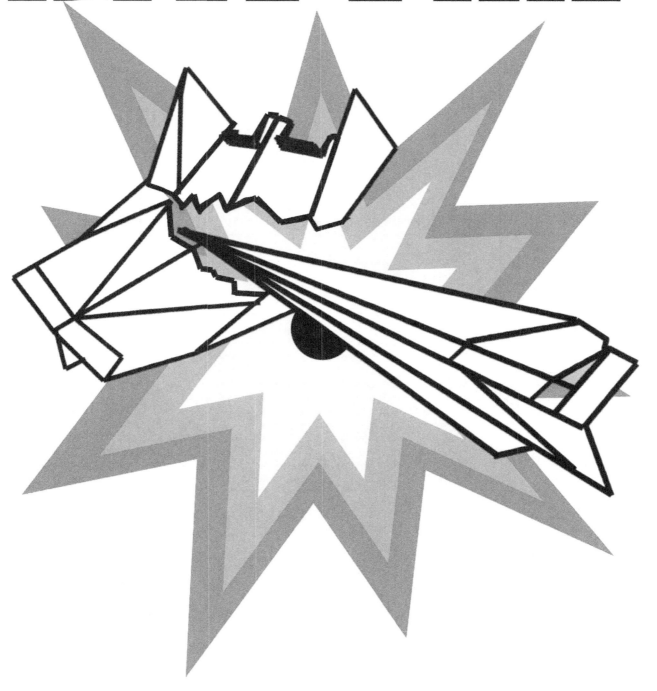

MISSION 1

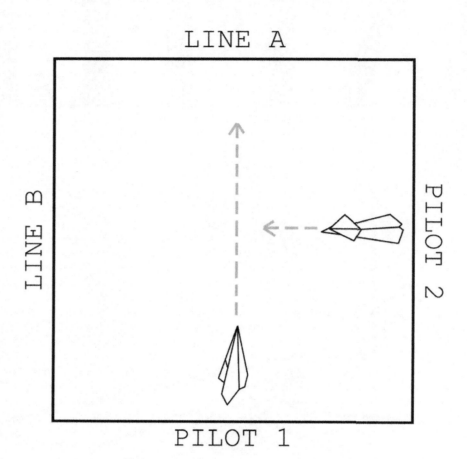

LINE A

LINE B

PILOT 2

PILOT 1

Mark off a square around 20x20ft (6x6m).
PILOT 1, from behind the line, tries to
throw their plane across LINE A. If
successful, PILOT 1 gets one point. However,
PILOT 2, from behind the line, throws their
plane at the same time to prevent PILOT 1
from crossing the line. If PILOT 2 hits
PILOT 1's plane and prevents it from
crossing the line, PILOT 2 receives 3
points. After each round, the PILOTS switch
positions. The winner is the first pilot to
a score of 9.

SCOREBOARD

Iron Ninja	**VS.**	Sky Shark

PILOT 1	round 1	round 2	round 3	round 4	round 5	round 6	round 7	round 8	round 9	WINNER
C.B.	1	1	3	0	3	0	0	0	1	Iron Ninja
PILOT 2										
T.J.	0	1	0	3	0	3	0	1	0	

	VS.	

PILOT 1	round 1	round 2	round 3	round 4	round 5	round 6	round 7	round 8	round 9	WINNER
PILOT 2										

SCOREBOARD

	VS.	

PILOT 1	round 1	round 2	round 3	round 4	round 5	round 6	round 7	round 8	round 9	WINNER
PILOT 2										

	VS.	

PILOT 1	round 1	round 2	round 3	round 4	round 5	round 6	round 7	round 8	round 9	WINNER
PILOT 2										

SCOREBOARD

		VS.		

	round 1	round 2	round 3	round 4	round 5	round 6	round 7	round 8	round 9	WINNER
PILOT 1										
PILOT 2										

		VS.		

	round 1	round 2	round 3	round 4	round 5	round 6	round 7	round 8	round 9	WINNER
PILOT 1										
PILOT 2										

SCOREBOARD

	VS.	

PILOT 1	round 1	round 2	round 3	round 4	round 5	round 6	round 7	round 8	round 9	WINNER
PILOT 2										

	VS.	

PILOT 1	round 1	round 2	round 3	round 4	round 5	round 6	round 7	round 8	round 9	WINNER
PILOT 2										

SCOREBOARD

| | | VS. | | |

PILOT 1	round 1	round 2	round 3	round 4	round 5	round 6	round 7	round 8	round 9	WINNER
PILOT 2										

| | | VS. | | |

PILOT 1	round 1	round 2	round 3	round 4	round 5	round 6	round 7	round 8	round 9	WINNER
PILOT 2										

SCOREBOARD

	VS.	

PILOT 1	round 1	round 2	round 3	round 4	round 5	round 6	round 7	round 8	round 9	WINNER
PILOT 2										

	VS.	

PILOT 1	round 1	round 2	round 3	round 4	round 5	round 6	round 7	round 8	round 9	WINNER
PILOT 2										

MISSION 2

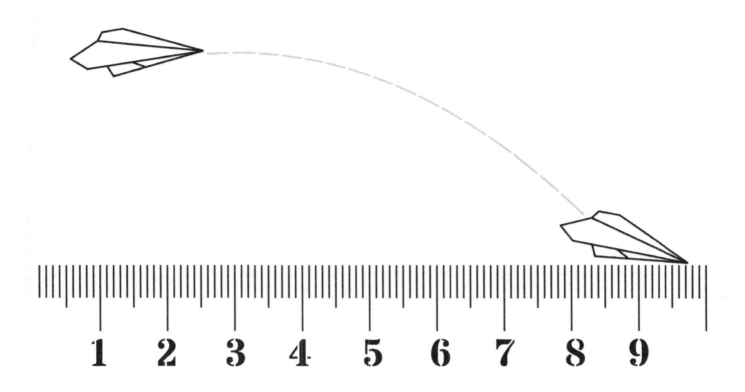

Pilot 1 and Pilot 2 each choose a plane. Each pilot gets three attempts to fly their plane as far as they can. Measure the distance of each of the three flights per pilot with a tape measure, and write the distance in the boxes given. Each pilot then adds their three distances together. The pilot with the largest number after the calculation is the winner.

SCOREBOARD

Drill Bit		**VS.**	Silver Raptor	

PILOT 1	DISTANCE 1	DISTANCE 2	DISTANCE 3	TOTAL
C.B.	15.2	5.5	11	31.7
PILOT 2	**DISTANCE 1**	**DISTANCE 2**	**DISTANCE 3**	**TOTAL**
T.J.	12.8	14.7	19.1	46.6

WINNER	NAME Tommy Johnson	PLANE Silver Raptor

		VS.		

PILOT 1	DISTANCE 1	DISTANCE 2	DISTANCE 3	TOTAL
PILOT 2	**DISTANCE 1**	**DISTANCE 2**	**DISTANCE 3**	**TOTAL**

WINNER	NAME	PLANE

SCOREBOARD

	VS.	

	VS.	

PILOT 1	DISTANCE 1	DISTANCE 2	DISTANCE 3	TOTAL
PILOT 2	DISTANCE 1	DISTANCE 2	DISTANCE 3	TOTAL

WINNER	NAME	PLANE

PILOT 1	DISTANCE 1	DISTANCE 2	DISTANCE 3	TOTAL
PILOT 2	DISTANCE 1	DISTANCE 2	DISTANCE 3	TOTAL

WINNER	NAME	PLANE

SCOREBOARD

	VS.	

PILOT 1	DISTANCE 1	DISTANCE 2	DISTANCE 3	TOTAL
PILOT 2	DISTANCE 1	DISTANCE 2	DISTANCE 3	TOTAL

WINNER	NAME	PLANE

	VS.	

PILOT 1	DISTANCE 1	DISTANCE 2	DISTANCE 3	TOTAL
PILOT 2	DISTANCE 1	DISTANCE 2	DISTANCE 3	TOTAL

WINNER	NAME	PLANE

SCOREBOARD

	VS.	

PILOT 1	DISTANCE 1	DISTANCE 2	DISTANCE 3	TOTAL
PILOT 2	DISTANCE 1	DISTANCE 2	DISTANCE 3	TOTAL

WINNER	NAME	PLANE

	VS.	

PILOT 1	DISTANCE 1	DISTANCE 2	DISTANCE 3	TOTAL
PILOT 2	DISTANCE 1	DISTANCE 2	DISTANCE 3	TOTAL

WINNER	NAME	PLANE

SCOREBOARD

| | | **VS.** | | |

PILOT 1	DISTANCE 1	DISTANCE 2	DISTANCE 3	TOTAL
PILOT 2	DISTANCE 1	DISTANCE 2	DISTANCE 3	TOTAL

WINNER	NAME	PLANE

| | | **VS.** | | |

PILOT 1	DISTANCE 1	DISTANCE 2	DISTANCE 3	TOTAL
PILOT 2	DISTANCE 1	DISTANCE 2	DISTANCE 3	TOTAL

WINNER	NAME	PLANE

SCOREBOARD

		VS.		

PILOT 1	DISTANCE 1	DISTANCE 2	DISTANCE 3	TOTAL
PILOT 2	DISTANCE 1	DISTANCE 2	DISTANCE 3	TOTAL

WINNER	NAME	PLANE

		VS.		

PILOT 1	DISTANCE 1	DISTANCE 2	DISTANCE 3	TOTAL
PILOT 2	DISTANCE 1	DISTANCE 2	DISTANCE 3	TOTAL

WINNER	NAME	PLANE

MISSION 3

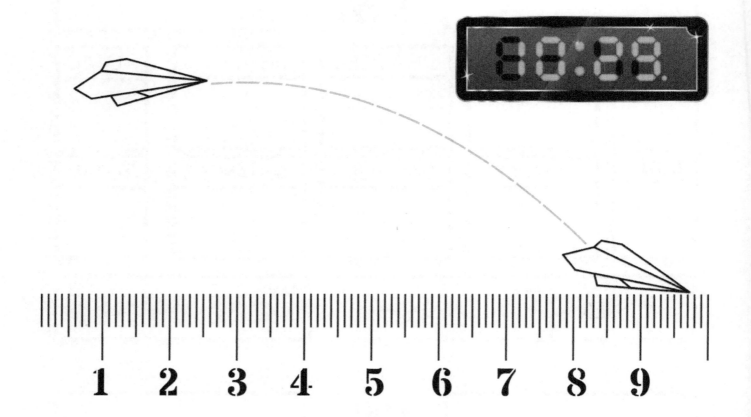

This is a solo flight mission with one pilot and one plane at a time. Throw the plane of choice and record its flight time using any sort of timing device. Once the plane lands, measure the distance from where you threw it to where it lands and record that on the sheets provided. Last, rank each plane on its performance from 1 to 10, ten being the best score. This will complete your last mission. Over and out, pilot.

SOLO FLIGHT LOG

PLANE NAME	FLIGHT TIME	FLIGHT DISTANCE	PLANE RANK
Frostbite	26.2 seconds	36ft 11m	8

SOLO FLIGHT LOG

PLANE NAME	FLIGHT TIME	FLIGHT DISTANCE	PLANE RANK

SOLO FLIGHT LOG

PLANE NAME	FLIGHT TIME	FLIGHT DISTANCE	PLANE RANK

SOLO FLIGHT LOG

PLANE NAME	FLIGHT TIME	FLIGHT DISTANCE	PLANE RANK

SOLO FLIGHT LOG

PLANE NAME	FLIGHT TIME	FLIGHT DISTANCE	PLANE RANK

SOLO FLIGHT LOG

PLANE NAME	FLIGHT TIME	FLIGHT DISTANCE	PLANE RANK

TIPS & TRICKS

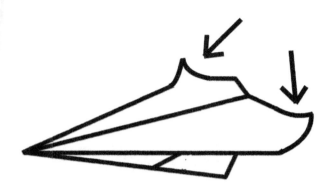

If you want the plane to go up, slightly bend the back wings up. If you want it to go down, bend them slightly down.

If you want the plane to go faster and further, add tape or a paper clip to keep it from opening and to add weight.

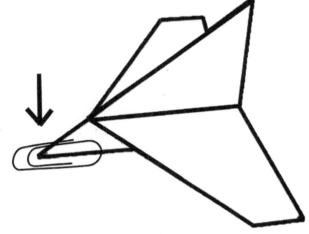

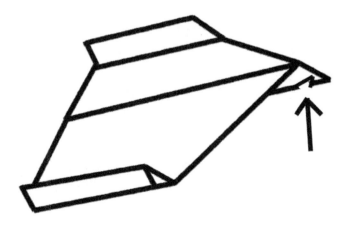

If you want a better launch, cut a small cut at the bottom of the nose and use a rubber band and your thumb to launch it.

Do you want more paper planes to color, fold, and fly? Check out this book by scanning the QR code.

Printed in Great Britain
by Amazon